Lieutenant Enloe Wanted Us to See Something Else Before We Left . . .

He motioned toward the dry, unweeded grass of the next-door lot. "This is where we found the teeth. See up there?" He pointed to the second-floor window just above us. "That's her bedroom. We figure she threw the teeth out when she thought we were going to search the house on Friday. We got one body without any teeth."

"What would she do with the teeth?" Tim Frawley, from the DA's office, asked.

"Hard to ID somebody without dental work. It's going to be hard to ID these bodies anyway. They're in bad shape." Enloe grinned. He knew Dorothea Montalvo Puente's past record by that time. "Besides, some of them were gold teeth."

Books by William P. Wood

Rampage
Gangland
Fugitive City
Court of Honor*
The Bone Garden*
Stay of Execution**

*Published by POCKET BOOKS
**Forthcoming from POCKET BOOKS

THE BONE GARDEN

THE SACRAMENTO BOARDINGHOUSE MURDERS

William P. Wood

POCKET BOOKS

New York   London   Toronto   Sydney   Tokyo   Singapore

An *Original* Publication of POCKET BOOKS

POCKET BOOKS, a division of Simon & Schuster Inc.
1230 Avenue of the Americas, New York, NY 10020

ISBN: 0-671-68638-0

First Pocket Books printing April 1994

10 9 8 7 6 5 4 3 2 1

POCKET and colophon are registered trademarks of
Simon & Schuster Inc.

Cover photo by UPI/Bettmann

Printed in the U.S.A.

Old cases sometimes come back at you.

Anyone who has been in criminal law has had it happen to them. The unexpected phone call. The fugitive arrested in a border city. The jail escapee caught during a robbery. The witness found dead.

Then the cops or the DA or a defense lawyer want to talk to you about something you did or didn't do years before.

The material contained in this book comes from police reports, evidence adduced at trial and at pretrial hearings, and conversations I had with various individuals connected to the case. Although this book is a factual account of a true story, certain events and dialogue have been reconstructed based on these sources.

When I left the Sacramento County District Attorney's Office in California after five years in 1982, I hoped I had heard the last of Dorothea Montalvo Puente. I had just sent her to prison for five years for robbing and drugging elderly people. I was appalled at the coldblooded way this sweet-looking, grandmotherly woman had deceived six victims and nearly killed another.

Then a family came forward and told me she had murdered their mother.

I thought I might hear about Dorothea Puente again.

It was November 1988 when I picked up a newspaper, read my own name, and saw that a body had been dug up in a yard downtown.

Then I saw the landlady's name. I was sick at heart. It was six years later, and eight more people had died. Nothing had been done to stop Puente. When she got out of prison on my cases, she had started killing again.

And I remembered the first victim, because I had never stopped thinking about her.

Her name was Ruth Munroe.

THE
BONE
GARDEN

Prologue

April 27, 1982

THE WOMAN LAY ON HER SIDE IN THE UPSTAIRS BEDROOM. SHE wore a pink nightgown. It was night outside and the lights were on in the room. The woman's eyes were open and she was trying to move.

Ruth Munroe had struggled to turn over, raise her hand, open her mouth to scream ever since she heard the voices downstairs. But she couldn't move at all. She could only stare at the wall.

She strained to hear who was downstairs. Sometimes her daughter Rosemary, Rosie she called her, came to visit. But for the last few nights it had been her son Bill, stopping by 1426 F Street after work to see how she was.

Ruth fought frantically to say something Bill would hear. Her mouth wouldn't open.

She had been drugged. She knew that. She had been working in a pharmacy at Gemco for ten years. She knew drugs and how they worked. This paralysis was unnatural. Someone had put something in her food.

Inwardly Munroe cringed. For the last three days she

1

hadn't eaten any solid food. All she had had were crème de menthe cocktails mixed by Dorothea. It will soothe you, Dorothea had said softly, it will make you feel better.

Ruth tried to cry out and failed again. She recognized Dorothea's voice and now she heard Bill's, too. He had come to see her, to make sure she was, as she had heard Dorothea tell him, getting better.

There's nothing wrong with me, she wanted to shout. She and Dorothea lived alone in the house. Ruth cursed herself as she lay paralyzed. She had moved in with Dorothea only a few weeks earlier. They had planned to go into business together, catering parties. It was something to fill Ruth's retirement.

She tried to talk. She had to talk, to get help from Bill.

She had her family to live for, grandchildren she loved. She didn't want to die.

The bedroom door opened. Ruth heard only one person come in. It was not Dorothea. Ruth knew those deliberate footsteps.

Bill sat down on the bed. He leaned over and spoke to her. "How are you, Mom?" he asked quietly.

Ruth tried to say something, anything.

Bill stroked her shoulder. "Everything's going to be okay. You're going to get better. Believe me."

Ruth twisted and writhed futilely inside her mind.

Bill was nearer. She could see his worried face, the dark brown hair, mustache. He said comfortingly, "Dorothea's going to look after you."

He kissed her. Ruth felt a tear roll down her cheek, from her open right eye. When he got up and left, she lay still on the bed, the tears dropping slowly.

Ruth must have slept or lost consciousness. Time passed. When she opened her eyes again, she was still on her side. The bedroom was dark, though, and the street outside utterly quiet. It felt like it was deep in the night or early morning.

Then the bedroom door opened. Ruth tried to squeeze against the wall, away from Dorothea who came resolutely to the bed, sat down, and with strong, determined hands, turned her on her back.

Dorothea was saying something. In the half-light from the hallway, her white hair was stark, her glasses dark, and Ruth realized Dorothea was swearing obscenely.

Roughly, Dorothea pulled Ruth's head up with one hand.

Ruth quavered. In her other hand, Dorothea was forcing a glass of sweet-tasting, minty liquid down Ruth's throat.

PART 1

"That corpse you planted last year in your garden,
"Has it begun to sprout? Will it bloom this year?
"Or has the sudden frost disturbed its bed?
"O keep the Dog far hence, that's friend to men,
"Or with his nails he'll dig it up again!"

T. S. Eliot,
The Waste Land

1

On Saturday morning, November 12, 1988, the crowd started gathering early across the street from the gray-blue gingerbread Victorian house at 1426 F Street in downtown Sacramento, California.

The crowd was larger than the day before, when it had first formed, drawn by the news that a body had been found in the backyard of the house. From across the street, held back by police barricades, the crowd could see that the two-story house was already festively decorated for Christmas and Thanksgiving.

On the dim, wet morning, the police floodlights were finally turned off after illuminating the house and yard all night. The police guard remained stoically in front of the brick and wrought-iron fence that framed the yard of 1426 F Street. More Sacramento city police officers, more diggers, more trucks, more coroner's deputies would be arriving soon.

And the crowd—restless, chattering, some holding umbrellas or pieces of plastic over their heads in the light rain—hoped to glimpse a shrouded shape or body bag being lugged from the backyard. All of the crowd—men, women, the crying or laughing children—wanted also to see the woman who ran 1426 F Street as a board-and-care home for the sick, drunk, and crazy.

Many people in the crowd knew about Dorothea Puente. Some had lived briefly at 1426 F Street, then left or been thrown out. They moved among the crowd, spreading tales of the tyrannical woman. She alternately cared for them and terrorized them. The former tenants and people who had heard other, more terrible rumors, all shivered with loathing and anticipation. For a long time many of them had believed people were dying strangely behind the gray walls, the high windows, the wrought-iron fence at 1426 F Street.

Every so often, Puente peered down from a second-story window at the crowd and the TV news trucks wedged tightly into the street.

By 8:00 A.M. the police had returned in force. They planned to dig up the entire L-shaped yard that ran from the driveway of 1426 F Street, around the house in a narrow course to the right, and ended against the next-door neighbor's wooden fence.

The long police barricades kept the growing crowd, somewhere near three hundred, across the street. The whole block of F Street was closed off at either end. The loud rumble of TV trucks' generators, a backhoe working the yard, and the massed voices thickened the air. The rain that had started on Friday, Veterans Day, tapered into a persistent dreary drizzle, fanned by a cold wind from the gray sky.

Inside 1426 F Street only a few tenants remained. Some had left when the police began seriously asking questions the day before. But Puente stayed. She was up early, around six, and ate a simple meal of eggs and toast. She was agitated and started drinking, too. Although she hated drunks, Puente often drank heavily, mostly in private, sometimes in bars, but usually only with people she trusted, like the man who joined her for breakfast, Mervin John McCauley. He was her longtime friend and sometime victim. They had vodka and orange juice cocktails.

They ate in the second floor kitchen, separated from the tenants who had their own stove downstairs. McCauley was like Puente, in his early sixties. He had a scraggly gray beard, and his thin body trembled because he was an antique alcoholic. He waved his bandaged left hand and chain-smoked as they drank and talked.

It was an uncomfortable morning for them both. They could hear the people outside and the loud noise, the men moving around the yard and the machinery. Puente swore to McCauley. Her face was still unnaturally tight from a recent cosmetic operation so she looked like she was half-grimacing. She wore a blue dress. Her white hair, neatly pinned back, and her glasses combined to make her look kindly.

Puente kept getting up to refill their glasses. McCauley was little help. She had to do something soon.

The police had already found one body in the backyard. It was, the police discovered, an elderly woman, wrapped in cloth and a blanket, secured with duct tape. Puente knew the woman's name was Leona Carpenter.

"I told them I didn't know anything," Puente said defiantly to McCauley. "I didn't bury anyone."

McCauley nodded vigorously. He liked Puente and agreed with anything she said. "That's right, Dorothea. You don't know anything about it. That's the truth."

Puente sat down. She had been getting Carpenter's Social Security checks for some time and had placed orders for shoes in Carpenter's name long after the woman was dead. The police would find this out, Puente knew, and much more.

She had been taken to the police department Friday afternoon. They asked her about the dead body, about other missing tenants. She indignantly said she knew nothing and anyone who was missing would turn up alive and well soon.

She and McCauley had been put together, alone, in an

interview room. The police, Puente knew, were hoping one of them would say something incriminating to the other.

But she and her old drinking companion only lamented the destruction of the backyard flower beds, and she worried aloud whether the police would tear up her carefully laid down cement driveway. It was, she and McCauley agreed, terrible to have so much upheaval so close to Thanksgiving.

While they ate breakfast, the other tenants prudently stayed away, aware of Puente's sudden flashes of temper and her propensity to slap or punch anyone who angered her. McCauley had been slugged several times, cursed at, but he remained friendly to Puente.

"I better go get dressed," Puente said, shoving the soiled dishes aside. McCauley made no move to clear up. "I want you to be ready in a little while," she said.

McCauley, smoke curled around him, nodded. "Anytime you say, Dorothea. I'm all set to go."

Puente went upstairs to her bedroom. She had at least one great secret from the police that drove her that morning.

She knew that within a short time, if they kept digging, they would find six more bodies buried around the compact yard. Already she knew the police were trying to solve a puzzle and it would draw them on to other secrets of hers.

They had come on Friday looking for a missing tenant named Bert Montoya, but when they started poking around in the backyard, the body they did uncover was too old, too slight, to be the burly Montoya.

So over that last breakfast, Puente and McCauley got ready to take a bold step. Time for Dorothea Puente was running very short and she had none to waste.

Her bedroom was cluttered but orderly. There was a satinlike coverlet on the bed, shelves of paperback westerns and mysteries on one wall. She started dressing. Audacity had served her all her life. How else could she have buried seven people around the small yard only a block from the old Governor's Mansion, five blocks from the county District Attorney's office, practically within sight of the white state capitol dome itself?

How else could she, ex-con, ex-hooker, have run a boardinghouse in violation of the law right under the noses of federal parole agents, state probation officers, the social service agencies who sent her tenants?

As she carefully dressed, hearing the boisterous noise outside, Puente knew the bodies about to be unearthed were only a few feet from a busy street, in a bustling residential neighborhood, in plain view of dozens of people who passed 1426 F Street every day.

But appearances and deception had always been a key to how Dorothea Puente lived anyway.

She had yellow and white bottles of Giorgio Beverly Hills cosmetics and perfume on her dressing bureau. She applied them studiously, watching her face in the mirror, critically studying how the face lift had coarsened and stretched her mouth.

Then she put on a pink dress, purple pumps, combed her thick, stylishly set white hair. Everything she wore that morning, from her feet to her hair was paid for by her tenants, living and dead, without their knowledge. She added a red wool overcoat and took a purple rolled up umbrella with her.

Into her purse she dropped a little over $3,000, all she had around the house. In a single month of tipping cabdrivers for trips around Sacramento, she had once spent up to $2,000. Her own Social Security income was only about $600 a month.

Puente got up, finishing quickly. Lying around the bedroom were tins of butter cookies, just as there were downstairs. She had been filling them with clothing and canteen supplies of candy and cigarettes for mailing to old friends at the California Institution for Women in Frontera. But that morning, with the police already back to digging, there was no time to finish packing the tins.

She gave herself a final survey in the mirror. Dressed and expensively perfumed, Puente saw that she looked like a slightly too corpulent grandmother. Her glasses gave her a stern disciplinarian's gaze. Only her eyes, black and hard behind the glasses, hinted at the stark truth beneath the unthreatening veneer of her appearance.

The house trembled with the thudding of machinery near its walls, and the cacophonous voices were louder. Puente hurried outside.

Twenty or more men and women in black or drab overalls stamped either POLICE or CORONER on the back, swarmed around the backyard. Their high boots were muddy, their shovels busy. The lush flower beds in the center of the yard were gone, the newly planted fruit trees uprooted. A small gazebo a few feet farther up the yard had been moved, and men were starting to dismantle a metal toolshed at the far end of the yard. Heaps of dark, alluvial-smelling dirt lay everywhere. Too many people were crammed into the narrow space as the backhoe noisily worked. At the side of the house, Puente stood silently, umbrella hooked over one arm, and watched.

Detective John Cabrera, who had come the day before, strolled toward her. He had on a blue windbreaker and jeans, and his legs were spattered with mud. He was as polite, casual as he had been Friday morning when he came searching for Montoya. They chatted. They agreed it was very noisy and confusing.

The makeshift tent erected over most of the backyard to shield any evidence from the rain, consisted of a plastic sheet stretched over bare wood, and in the morning's drizzle and breezes, it sighed and crackled.

Puente moved a few feet up the driveway, away from the brick and wrought-iron fence in front. The crowd and alert reporters spotted her, and a murmuring grew across the street. Puente disdainfully avoided looking at the crowd or lights. She had bragged in the past to some of the people in the crowd about being famous. "I was in Hiroshima when they dropped the atom bomb," she told people. "I lived through the Bataan Death March," she told others. "I made movies with Rita Hayworth. I'm a medical doctor. I'm a lawyer," she said proudly.

Now as real fame reached out for her, Puente refused to acknowledge it. She grew anxious, nervous. She tapped her foot.

It was nearly 9:00 A.M. Cabrera and his partner, a bigger older man, Terry Brown, were talking and pointing around the yard. They did not believe her, Puente was sure. Cabrera had said she was lying Friday. She tapped her foot more quickly. The digging was too intense. She couldn't wait.

Puente went over to Cabrera and asked him if she could walk to the Clarion Hotel across the street, about a block away. She wanted to see her nephew, who worked there. "I want to get away from all this noise and everything that's going on for a few minutes." Puente sighed. "I'd like a quiet cup of coffee."

John Cabrera had been a police officer for fifteen years. He had worked Homicide/Assaults long enough to know a con when he heard one. He wanted to arrest the kindly little old lady beside him right then, but his superiors and the DA said there wasn't enough evidence. Keep digging and looking, they said. So Cabrera, who had dark hair and a mustache and an exuberant manner, listened to Puente as if he believed her. He examined her. She did actually seem worn out.

He left her and went up the yard to ask Lieutenant Joe Enloe about the request. Enloe, one of the supervising city cops on the scene, was balding, heavyset, and had on a white shapeless raincoat. The two cops talked briefly.

Cabrera came back to Puente. She asked him sharply, "Am I under arrest, Mr. Cabrera?"

Grinning sheepishly to put her at ease, Cabrera said, "No, you're not under arrest. And you can go to the hotel for a couple of minutes."

"Thank you. I'd like you to help me get through these reporters and people," Puente said politely, purse in one hand, hooking the umbrella over her wrist. "I can't do it by myself."

The two of them set off. John McCauley will come by, too, Puente said. Cabrera moved authoritatively, halting cars,

13

taking her arm sometimes as they walked over rough patches of sidewalk. If he couldn't arrest her, Cabrera was determined to know where she was that critical morning. He would drop her off personally at the hotel.

They chatted about the weather, minor matters, like old friends, both solicitous and courteous to the other. A passerby would never have known that Cabrera had accused Puente of murder less than twenty-four hours earlier.

They walked past the old Governor's Mansion on the corner of 12th Street, a major tourist attraction, then across another street to the boxlike and ivy-covered Clarion Hotel. The gray sky was heavy with more rain as Cabrera left Puente and saw McCauley meet her. He watched them both go into the hotel to meet Puente's nephew, really her landlord at 1426 F Street and an old friend.

Cabrera walked back to the digging. He was positive something terrible had happened at F Street and more than ever convinced Dorothea Puente was involved. Enloe asked him when he got back if she was at the hotel now and Cabrera nodded. He went back to checking the yard for suspicious depressions in the soil.

Shortly before ten, after Puente had been gone about twenty minutes, Cabrera heard a shout from one of the digging groups. The other cops stopped, the backhoe idled. In another shallow grave like the one he had found Friday, Cabrera and his partner Brown saw a second wrapped body being uncovered. It too was buried about eighteen inches down, beside the wooden fence that ran along the lefthand side of the narrow backyard.

As he stared down, Cabrera saw that this body, like the first, was swaddled in cloth, dirt-covered, wrapped like a crude latter-day mummy, with a whitish sprinkling of lime on the cloth. The whole neighborhood was called Alkali Flat because lime existed close to the topsoil. But this layer of lime looked like it had been deliberately spread over the body, either in hopes of hastening decomposition or disguising any odor.

Cabrera's heart sank at the sight of the lime and the

14

second wrapped body. Simultaneously he, Brown, and Enloe realized there was suddenly abundant reason to arrest Dorothea Montalvo Puente. One body the wrong age, size, and sex for a missing tenant was too hard to pin on Puente. A second body meant there was a lot more going on at 1426 F Street.

Cabrera took off running to the Clarion Hotel. At Puente's old lady's pace, the two of them had taken ten minutes to walk there. He covered the distance in no time at full speed, cursing as he went.

He looked in the lobby dining area, the buffet. She wasn't there. Nor was McCauley or her "nephew" and landlord, Ricardo Odorica. In fact, Cabrera learned that Odorica didn't even work Saturdays.

With a sinking certainty, Cabrera checked the rest of the hotel, the grounds, the block around it, but he knew Puente was gone.

He ran back to 1426 F Street and put out a call for her arrest. She had about a half hour's start. Cabrera knew from experience with fleeing suspects that thirty minutes was a long lead.

At the crime scene as the news spread, there was a lot of swearing and anger among the cops, which spread back downtown to the police department, through the ranks of captains to the chief. To make the episode more embarrassing, Cabrera remembered he had been captured on film by the photographers and TV, gallantly escorting the white-haired suspect away from 1426 F Street.

But Cabrera's personal problem became Sacramento's shame. Within twenty-four hours a nationwide manhunt was begun for Dorothea Montalvo Puente, her pre-facelift, thinner, more bug-eyed driver's license photo spread on newspaper front pages, on the TV network news. The Sacramento Police Department was ridiculed for letting her get away.

In seventy-two hours, intense searches went on for Puente in Stockton, Garden Grove, and Glendale, California. She was reportedly spotted in Las Vegas, Nevada. The Attorney

General of California, who was in Chihuahua for a law enforcement conference, made a personal appeal to the Mexican police for help in finding the fugitive. Puente, with relatives in Mexico, was rumored to have fled south. She had tried to do so before, in 1982, when facing criminal charges.

At 1426 F Street, by the start of the next week, seven bodies had been unearthed, in various stages of decomposition, indicating some had been buried up to a year, others less than a few months. One victim, found beneath a shrine to St. Francis of Assisi in the front yard, was curiously robed in a white sheet, like a specter, buried in a sitting pose. The body was missing its head, hands, and lower legs.

Puente had been revealed as that rarest of killers, a female serial murderer. She was rarer still because even at the start of the investigation, the police rightly believed she killed not from passion but for profit alone. Night after night her white-haired bespectacled, plumpish face appeared on TV. She was a celebrity, a freak, a homicidal grandmother.

As the hunt for her went on, no one knew who the seven victims buried at 1426 F Street were. Nor did anyone know if these were the only victims. There was no sign of how any of these people had died or even whether they had been murdered.

As for Puente herself, the woman behind the haunting image, the object of law enforcement's frantic search from one side of the border to the other, the prime suspect in an unknown number of murders committed in the heart of California's capital, she had vanished into thin air as the long Veterans Day weekend ended.

2

JOHN CABRERA HAD STARTED OUT THE DAY BEFORE THINKING HE was just doing his job, trying to allay the worries of two social workers about a missing, retarded Costa Rican native.

So on Friday, November 11, 1988, five people crowded into the small office of the Homicide/Assault section at the Sacramento Police Department. Because it was Veterans Day, the old granite building was quieter than usual, quiet enough to hear the wind and dripping rain outside.

Cabrera was joined by his partner, Terry Brown, and Jim Wilson, a federal parole agent. Beth Valentine and Judy Moise were from the Volunteers of America, Outreach Social Workers.

Cabrera was informally running the early morning meeting. Brown, in his mid-forties, smoking sometimes, half smiling, let his outgoing partner handle the two social workers. Valentine and Moise had become very persistent in the last few days, urging the cops to do something about Dorothea Puente and the way she was acting about a missing tenant.

17

Cabrera had Wilson check his file on Puente and tell them what he knew about the woman.

Wilson had only recently become Dorothea Puente's federal parole agent, and he had never met her. He said she had been placed on federal parole in 1978 for forging checks and had been contacted thirty-five times by federal parole agents since she was released from custody on California state criminal charges in 1985. Most of those contacts had been at the federal parole office downtown. But on fourteen occasions, he said, flipping the file pages, Puente had invited agents to inspect her living arrangements as a tenant at 1426 F Street. No agent ever submitted a report that she was running any kind of boardinghouse or had other tenants living with her or that she was supplementing her assistance income in any way.

"She's not allowed to," Wilson pointed out. The conditions of her federal parole restricted her travel, banned contact with other parolees, and very specifically prohibited her from being employed by the elderly or emotionally handicapped.

Moise, light-haired, intense, said to Cabrera, "She's violating her parole. She gets people's Social Security checks, and she's got Bert living with her." The missing man Valentine and Moise were worried about was Alvaro "Bert" Montoya and he was retarded and mentally ill.

Valentine and Moise could completely not hide their frustration. They had told another Sacramento cop all about Bert Montoya and their fears for his safety with Puente that week. Now for the two homicide detectives and federal agent, they repeated what they knew about Montoya.

Unfortunately, they didn't know everything that had happened to Bert since he moved in at 1426 F Street.

Montoya was born in Costa Rica. In his mid-fifties in 1988, he was fat, with gray hair and a whitish beard or sometimes only a mustache. He was one of the two hundred or so clients Valentine and Moise saw every month in downtown Sacramento. Montoya had been living at the

Volunteers of America Detoxification Center on Front Street since 1982, and it was there the two women met him.

There was a forlorn but endearing quality to Bert that made him stand out for Valentine and Moise. Moise had seen a great deal of suffering and despair since joining VOA in 1986. Her territory downtown embraced Alkali Flat and the darker, older part of the city, thick with old trees and old houses and fading elegance from the era when it had been the home of governors and flour barons.

The governors and barons were long gone. Hallucinating, shouting drunks, men and women with diseases, poorer workers struggling to live, had taken over the crumbling fine houses and seedy apartments.

Bert, though, was big, and genial, and fearful, as if he didn't understand what was happening to him. At the Detox Center he was a rarity, mentally ill instead of alcoholic. He was a poor soul and easy to like. He spoke English better some days than others. Since he was a teenager, Montoya had suffered from hallucinations, some that spoke to him. He was frightened by the large cemetery near the Detox Center. Demons were calling to him from the graveyard where Sacramento buried its illustrious dead. Sometimes Bert heard his own dead father urging him to kill himself, so they could be together.

What Cabrera and Brown heard that far in the meeting sounded like the story of many of the lunatics and transients prowling downtown. They were around one day, gone the next. There didn't seem much to get worked up about in the case of this one missing man.

But Valentine and Moise argued for Montoya. For nearly two years he had been their special project. They contacted twenty-eight agencies trying to clarify his various legal and financial problems. He had been adopted, in a way, by the Detox Staff.

Bert would wave to the staff when they left in the morning, pat them on the shoulder when they returned. The big, confused, genial man sometimes was given a King

Edward cigar. Bert enjoyed the cigars immensely, leaning back, grinning, acting like he was worth a million dollars when he smoked one.

His major problem, Valentine and Moise said, was that he was easily led. He would just go along with a situation until it became intolerable.

What happened to Bert in February 1988 seemed like a blessing. Although neither Valentine nor Moise knew it, it was in truth his death sentence.

The two social workers had heard about Dorothea Puente's boardinghouse. They brought Bert to 1426 F Street, and Puente fastened on him immediately, talking gently to him in Spanish. She comforted him. She acted like she cared about him. She told the social workers she could make Bert better.

"She gave him a room, a TV. She said she'd make Spanish meals for him," Moise told Cabrera. For several months, everything looked fine. Every time Valentine or Moise visited Bert at F Street, he looked better physically. His hair was cut and combed, his clothes clean. He was being medicated for a skin problem. He sounded less suspicious of people.

But in mid-August, something happened. Montoya showed up again at the Detox Center, angry, confused, saying he didn't want to stay at 1426 F Street anymore. Dorothea was being unkind to him.

The Detox staff couldn't make much of what Bert said beyond his unhappiness, and having no place else to put him, they convinced him to go back to F Street. They drove him there. His old friends never saw him again. It was August 16, 1988.

What Puente did to simpleminded, trusting Bert Montoya was replicated over and over with other victims. First she won his confidence. Then she secured his money. Finally, she got rid of him because he became too troublesome. Bert was wearing out his welcome as far as Puente was concerned.

Part of the problem, for Puente, was that outsiders kept checking up on Bert. Lucy Yokota from the Health Department, for example, saw Montoya regularly from June 1987 through June 1988 about his tuberculosis. She wanted to "eyeball" him every two weeks and kept up with his life closely. She noted that Bert got better once he moved in at 1426 F Street, becoming more fit and talkative.

But Puente was a different story. By June 1988, the Health Department decided Bert's TB was cured and stopped his medication. This was not good enough for Puente who warned Yokota to stop coming by 1426 F to see Bert. In April, Puente had called Yokota angrily and shouted that she didn't want anyone visiting Bert. She threatened to send him back to the Detox Center and then hung up.

Puente had found other uses for Bert and his large size. Sometime in August 1988, after he returned to F Street, Bert was ordered to help Puente and another tenant unload sixty-five bags of cement. Bert, acting under Puente's sharp orders, stacked bags under the stairs at the front of the house. When the truck driver delivering the cement tried to talk to Bert, Puente instantly prevented it. She said Bert was retarded and she was the only one who could talk to him.

Puente had already taken Bert to the Social Security office, listed herself as his substitute payee, and thus gained control over the monthly checks he received. She stood over him as he signed his name and she entered hers as a relative. Puente had also gotten control of a trust account for Bert at the Bank of America and used it as a personal slush fund for herself. Puente bought fruit cake, Giorgio cologne at $110 a bottle and clothing, all for herself.

Although she wanted to keep him away from the inquisitive eyes of health workers and Moise and Valentine, Puente had no problem if Bert was kept close to 1426 F Street and people she knew. She set up a monthly account of about $80 for him at Joe's Corner, the bar at the end of the 1400 block. Puente knew the owner very well. She was a regular there herself, and brought in bundles of checks made out to her sometimes totaling $2,000. She never, though, came to drink with any of her tenants. They were the business part of her life, and she separated recreation and business.

Bert used the monthly account Puente had doled out to him to buy two or three beers and burritos once or twice a week. He said little, and struck most patrons and the bartender as shy. There was one disturbing incident in early August, shortly before Bert tried to flee 1426 F Street. He came to the bar about eleven-thirty in the morning, had his beers and burritos, and then passed out. He had to be carried back, half a block, to 1426 F Street. It was as if Bert had suddenly been struck by the effects of some drug.

He never came to Joe's Corner again. When Puente, grandly flourishing a batch of checks, arrived several weeks later and was asked about the absent Bert, she said he had gone to Mexico. She told the bartender to cancel Bert's monthly account. Plainly, she didn't think he would return.

But Bert's last known contact with the world outside 1426 F Street was chilling. The mask of pleasant, kindly concern that Puente wore slipped and revealed something wicked.

On September 2, a young woman working in the Consumer Affairs Section at the Main Branch of the Sacramento Post Office got a startling call around ten-thirty in the morning. A man identified himself as Bert Montoya. He was frightened, stuttering, nervous as he spoke. Behind him the young woman could hear another voice, yelling and raging obscenely. "I'll put his goddamn ass out on the goddamn street," a female voice screamed.

"What's wrong?" the postal worker asked worriedly.

"She's got my Social Security check and she's yelling at me," Bert stuttered back fearfully. "I can't give you my phone number. I live at 1426 F Street."

Trying to take notes, the young postal worker strained to hear Bert over the yelling woman in the background. Bert said the manager where he lived had taken his Social Security check. He couldn't even write down anything the postal worker told him. The manager, screaming and raging, wouldn't let him have a pencil. He talked for five minutes,

around 1426. Christine P—
present," she said. "I've just bought [?]
Puente began weeping. "Moise immediately.
he had to contact Moise transferred to another social worker and
that Bert was being a ruse. Moise used a ruse, telling Puente
looking stricken and tired.

William P. Wood

Wilson o[n] [...]
what had happene[d] [...]

In mid-September, Mo[...]
Mexico," Puente said, to visit he[r] [...]
as highly unlikely. Bert had trouble navigati[ng] [...]
Alkali Flat and a transcontinental journey was far [...] d
him. "He'll be back in a few days," Puente assured Moise.

It was, Moise realized bitterly, just another of the
innumerable lies Dorothea Puente had told.

Near the end of September, still without a clue about
Bert's whereabouts, Moise again saw Puente. Puente was in
a fine mood, happy to help. Bert had made a great impression on her family in Mexico. He was a favorite of her sister
and brother-in-law, a respected banker.

"I want him to call me and tell me he's all right," Moise
insisted.

"I'll make sure he calls," Puente replied.

But there was no call then or later, when Moise returned.
"Bert's called me," Puente said. "He's doing just fine."

At first, Moise and Valentine believed that Puente had
unwisely sent the retarded Montoya to Mexico where he had
gotten lost or come to harm, and she was now hiding her
actions.

It could not, they told themselves, be more sinister than
that. Not that brisk, grandmotherly old woman. Not in the
middle of downtown Sacramento.

But on November 1, the social workers confronted
Puente. They found her on the front porch at 1426 F Street,

23

... Christmas
... ...stmas decorations had gone up
... 1426 F Street, including a macabre string of little
white Santa Claus heads along the length of a wooden
driveway fence. There were so many they looked like
shrunken trophy heads.

Moise said Bert could stay with Puente until Christmas,
but he had to contact her or Valentine and come back to
Sacramento.

"If we haven't heard from Bert by November seventh,
we'll report him missing to the police," Moise firmly told
Puente.

"I'll go to Mexico and bring him back myself," Puente
said stoutly. "I'll go Saturday. You can come back that
afternoon and see Bert."

But on Monday morning, Moise got a call at work from a
man who said he was Bert's brother-in-law. He was calling
from Utah and had driven through Sacramento Saturday
and picked Bert up.

Instantly suspicious, Moise demanded, "I want to talk to
him."

"He's under the weather, he's a little sick right now," the
man said. He went on to magnanimously decline Bert's
Social Security. "We don't take charity," he said to Moise.

Dorothea, he said, had wanted Bert to stay with her. And
Bert had very much wanted to stay. He'd had a tough fight
to convince Bert to leave on Saturday. The man hung up.

Moise relayed the information to Valentine. Neither of
them had ever heard of any Montoya relatives in Utah.
Then a letter purporting to be from the same brother-in-law
arrived, saying Bert would stay with him. It was mailed from
Reno, Nevada.

The whole thing looked wrong, as if Puente was still
trying to keep anyone from contacting Bert. Moise got on
the phone to Puente. After a long, almost reflective pause,

Puente repeated the same story as the mysterious "brother-in-law".

"I'm calling the police," Moise announced, fed up with the lies and false leads.

"Could you wait until three o'clock?" Puente asked.

"No," Moise snapped. She called the Sacramento Police Department and filed a missing person report on Bert Montoya. A patrol officer later came to see Moise and Valentine and took down their information. There was no question for the two social workers. Dorothea Puente knew that something terrible had happened to Bert.

The patrol officer, later on Monday morning, November 7, went to 1426 F Street and talked to Puente.

Cabrera had seen the patrol officer's report. He and Terry Brown realized that the odd call and the letter meant Puente had at least one accomplice in any criminal activity.

Wilson was perplexed. A tenant, like Montoya, living with Puente? Four parole agents over time had visited her and she had manipulated the inspections in such a way that they never realized that the two-story Victorian house at 1426 F Street had tenants on the ground floor.

The detectives also now had information that on November 7 Puente had gotten an elderly tenant, John Sharp, to lie to the police about Bert leaving in a pickup truck on Saturday. The old man, however, had managed to slip a note to the patrol officer: "She's making me lie," it said, and the fear was obvious in the words.

Cabrera had also heard from a sometime prostitute and heroin addict named Brenda Trujillo recently. Trujillo had known Puente from their common time in county jail in 1982 and had lived at 1426 F Street when she was out of prison. Cabrera and Brown had discounted Trujillo's venomous denunciations of Puente, however, because Trujillo herself was a suspect in a murder (although the investigation was dropped). But the ex-con had said people were dying at the quiet house and Puente was burying them on the property.

With all of this information, Cabrera and Brown decided to do what the two social workers wanted, check out the house and Puente themselves, look around the yard for anything resembling a grave. At the very least, Cabrera hoped the search would finally satisfy the bothersome VOA workers who were threatening to go higher in the police department if he didn't do something.

"Okay," Cabrera said cheerfully, "let's go take a look," and a little before 9:00 A.M. a small caravan drove the twenty or so peaceful city blocks from the police department to 1426 F Street. The only other traffic was headed toward the Veterans Day parade set to start later that morning.

3

THINGS COULDN'T HAVE STARTED OFF BETTER WHEN THE SMALL
expedition got to 1426 F Street. Moise and Valentine,
concerned they might spook Puente, peeled off and parked a
little distance from the house. Cabrera, Brown, and Wilson
went up the front porch. It was cold outside, the sky leaden.
Cabrera knocked on a paper Thanksgiving turkey stuck in
the center of the door.

Puente appeared, smiling, in the doorway. She had on a
blue dress with white dots, and a white sweater. She was
courtly and soft-spoken, her plump little hands fiddling with
the edges of the sweater. How could anyone who looked so
sweet be guilty of even the hint of what Moise and Valentine
suspected?

After making the introductions quickly, Cabrera went
into the riskiest part of his sales pitch. He wanted her to
agree to let them look around the property, talk to the
tenants, try to get some idea where Bert Montoya might be.
To Cabrera's relief, Puente, who could have ordered them
off the property, only asked, "How can I help you?"

They all went inside where it was warmer. It was also stuffy, only a few lights on in the crowded living room against the dark morning. Puente offered them coffee, candy. They all declined.

Unconsciously, it was hard for Cabrera and the two other men to deal with Puente like a usual suspect. Nothing in their experience prepared them for her. She was kindly, cooperative, looked old, frail, and even timid. Making her out a killer or con artist didn't add up.

Now that they were in the door, Wilson dropped the hammer a little on her. He told her she had violated her federal parole by taking in tenants.

Puente nodded, arms folded. "I know it's wrong," she said contritely.

They walked through the living room toward the kitchen. Wilson advised Puente that her parole would be revoked. She took the news calmly. In the kitchen Cabrera noticed a wall calendar hanging on the door. It was almost too obvious. In early November, jotted in, was a note that Bert had gone to Mexico.

Cabrera turned to Puente. He asked about Bert. She was still calm. She said she hadn't seen him since September. Then, a little later during the house tour, Puente changed her story and told Cabrera she had gone to Tijuana to pick Bert up on November 4.

Both homicide detectives were interested in the number of pill bottles scattered throughout the kitchen. There were many bottles—sauces, liquor, medication—on tables, on counters. They had seen more pill bottles in the living room. Cabrera found a small cupboard in the kitchen; the rows of medications the tenants were taking in it.

Casually chatting with Puente to put her at ease, Cabrera also increased the pressure. "Now, Dorothea, I see you've got some felonies on your record. Drugs, forgery, things like that."

Puente nodded. "I did those things, but they're in the past. I'm trying to straighten my life out."

The three men split up and began talking to the six

28

tenants about Bert and another missing man, Ben Fink. No one had any information.

Cabrera was rapidly concluding that the visit was futile. Finally, after an hour in the stale, tired atmosphere of what felt like a run-down nursing home, he asked Puente, "Dorothea, you mind if we check around outside? Maybe do a little digging?"

"No, no," Puente said helpfully. "Go ahead. There's nothing there." Just be careful of the new plantings, she said.

Cabrera, Brown, and Wilson returned to their cars, got metal probes and shovels, brought along as precautions, and went up the driveway into the backyard. Puente hovered like a bird around them. Over the wind came the faint sounds of drums and trombones and a cheering crowd as the parade passed the capitol building.

Cabrera complimented Puente on the lush, neat backyard. He was intrigued, like Brown, by the brick-bordered planter in the yard's center, just above the end of the concrete driveway, the stand of freshly planted small fruit trees in it, and thin, amateurishly poured cement around the trees. A metal toolshed was worth looking at, too. So was a tiny gazebo crowded into the upper part of the yard and an old sink turned into a planter beside the wood fence.

Trees, small plants, stones, statues, all made good unobtrusive markers for anything buried beneath them.

Peering around, Cabrera and Brown noted the ivy and flower beds arranged tightly in the narrow yard, with more flowerpots standing on the rain-damp cement, waiting to be planted. Cabrera knew Puente had a local reputation as an energetic and assiduous gardener, often working in the predawn darkness, digging and planting, tending the flowers and trees around the house, dragging heavy fertilizer bags behind her.

Cabrera was careful not to knock over any of the stone figures of cats on the cramped brick pathway between the flower beds. Puente stood, arms folded, face impassive, as he talked to Brown and Wilson, pointing out places around the yard to check. Everything was being done calmly, almost casually.

Once more, Cabrera asked Puente if it was all right to do a little digging.

"Go ahead," she said, nodding. Cabrera, as he turned to push his metal probe into the soil, wondered how a woman who had just been told by her parole agent that she would probably go back to prison, could be so cool.

The whole scene was incongruous, the grandmother waiting as cops poked in her flower beds for corpses, the gingerbread house so neat on the outside and so musty inside, concealing who knew what horrors. George Bush had just become President, people were starving in Sudan, Stanford was going to play UCLA in the Rose Bowl the next day. How could anything be very wrong at 1426 F Street in downtown Sacramento?

The fact was that Sacramento itself was a mix of incongruities, home of the legislature, cosmopolitan with a large airport, a cathedral, ballet and symphony, but also with nearby rice fields and almond packing plants. The city had three hundred thousand people, the county another seven hundred thousand. In the summer it could sweat for weeks over a hundred degrees, and in the winter, shiver under sheets of endless rain.

Sacramento was almost one hundred fifty years old in 1988, a Gold Rush boomtown that had become the state capital after rough bargaining. It had a busy port and yet lived in fear that the two great rivers that bisected it, the American and Sacramento, could flood it despite elaborate levees.

By 1988, Dorothea Puente had spent almost forty years, off and on, in Sacramento. Something about its deceptive appearance, its lust for past and future glamor and importance, must have attracted her predatory nature.

In fact, Sacramento was also a place of overlapping police jurisdictions. City police, county sheriffs, state police, federal agents, all worked in the city or county and frequently did not communicate on important matters.

Puente instinctively understood the possibilities in a tattered web of interlocking responsibilities. The Social Security Administration downtown might never talk to the city police. The federal court might never exchange information about her with the police or social service agencies. She could move about with ease.

She could in fact get away with murder.

The three men had been digging for a while. Puente stood in the cool wind, her white hair plucked at, but otherwise immovable.

Hitting on shallow roots in the thick, riverbed dirt that lay under Sacramento, Cabrera was growing tired.

A grizzled face appeared at the second-floor window over him. It was Mervin John McCauley, cigarette in hand. He called down to the three men, "You might find some garbage buried in there."

"Like what?" Cabrera called back.

"You know. Garbage. Junk." McCauley's face vanished from the window.

Cabrera and Brown chuckled. It was an odd thought, though. Why bury garbage in the backyard when the city picked up trash at the sidewalk every week? Why make sure the police know about it?

Wilson was digging in the upper left hand side of the yard, near the fence. Another lot, empty and weed-clotted, butted up against 1426 F. On either side of the property were aging Victorians, all occupied, and all able to see into the cramped backyard. Bury people out here? The idea was idiotic.

Then Wilson called to Cabrera. His shovel had struck something, and he wanted one of the detectives to dig for him, in case it was important.

Going to Wilson's shallow hole, Cabrera bent down and started digging. Brown paused and watched. Soon Cabrera hit what felt like a hidden tree root. It was, he saw looking closer, an object mixed with white powder, maybe the lime of Alkali Flat. A small fruit tree grew nearby, like a marker.

Cabrera was puzzled, so he turned the dark soil over more carefully, calling Brown over. It was not a root. Cloth, really only rags, was coming up from the narrow hole. He reached down and began plucking the material out, bits and pieces coming off in his hand. He could not tell what it was. Brown didn't know, either. It was dry and translucent and Cabrera could see the thin, elusive sun through the stuff when he held it up.

Just then, he realized he had not been pulling up bits of cloth, but dried skin. He poked down with his shovel. He uncovered a bone, white, still partly covered with skin, in some kind of shoe.

From the side of the house, as the three men turned to her, Dorothea Puente held her hands to her face, over her mouth. It was, Cabrera first thought, a gesture of shock, her eyes wide behind her glasses. From then until the day of her sentencing, it was the only surprise she ever expressed publicly.

As Brown and Wilson checked the find, Cabrera knew that this skeletalized body, whether human or animal, had been in the ground far too long to be Bert Montoya.

"We've got something to talk about, Dorothea," Cabrera said.

4

On Saturday, November 12, after she had gotten to the Clarion Hotel, and was satisfied Detective Cabrera had left, Puente sent McCauley outside to see if any police officers were nearby. McCauley saw no one. He was an odd sight, skulking quickly around the hotel, smoking, bandaged hand, baseball cap on his gray hair, watery eyes behind tinted glasses.

When she was certain the police weren't watching her, Puente and McCauley immediately took a cab to Tiny's Lounge, a bar she knew in West Sacramento, across the Sacramento River.

The bar was not far from the Port of Sacramento, surrounded by truck stops, gas stations, busy freeways. Early morning drinkers liked it. Puente led McCauley to a table in the nearly empty bar. It was only nine-thirty, and back at F Street, the second body had not yet been uncovered.

She ordered and swiftly drank four vodkas and grapefruit

juice to calm down. McCauley limited himself to one beer. They stayed together about fifteen minutes, talking, brooding, Puente lamenting all the wrongs that were being done to her. McCauley later denied knowing what Puente was going to do, but he certainly didn't think she was going sightseeing in an industrial neighborhood on a gloomy holiday weekend.

They said their farewells. Puente had been good to McCauley, allowing him the rare privilege of living on the second floor of 1426 F with her, drinking with her, sharing meals. No other tenant was treated like that. They wished each other well as Puente got a cab for McCauley.

He left Tiny's Lounge around ten. Puente went back to the bar and called a second cab for herself. She had been planning what to do ever since Friday morning, through the long, restless night splashed with floodlights at 1426 F.

A Capitol City Co-Op cab arrived to pick her up. She told the cabbie to take her south, to Stockton, a city she knew fairly well, about forty miles away. It would cost her $70, but that's what she said she wanted to do.

The cabbie settled her into the backseat and turned south, heading for I-5. The woman he drove impressed him, umbrella at her side, as genteel, fashionable, almost regal.

Hurrying south, the rain starting again, Dorothea Puente saw green pastures and huge electrical towers along the freeway. The money she had with her was all she possessed in the world. She had lost control of the thousands of dollars of checks that came to the tenants every month at F Street.

She had told Detective Cabrera many lies in the last twenty-four hours. When he asked how long Bert Montoya had lived with her, she blurted out two months. She told Cabrera that Bert didn't want to see Judy Moise anymore; she bothered him. And she said that Bert's brother-in-law had come and taken him away the weekend before.

"If I had anything to hide," Puente blustered to Cabrera as they sat in the very tiny police interview room Friday morning, right after the first body was found, "I wouldn't have let you dig around the yard."

Cabrera, windbreaker off, in a shortsleeved shirt said quickly, "I think Bert's dead."

"He's not dead," she answered back as quickly.

"We found a body. I think, Dorothea, if we dig, there's others. What about Bert?"

"Sir, I have never killed anybody," she said, and told the man only an arm's length across the little table, how much she cared for poor Bert Montoya. "I haven't killed anyone. My conscience isn't bothering me," she said. Then to add weight to her claim, she told the detective she'd seen Bert several times in the week before he left with his brother-in-law.

Bert, she said, will come back. "I believe in God, and I know he's going to show up."

But Detective Cabrera didn't seem to believe her. He kept pressing on. He knew they would find more bodies, he knew Bert was dead, he knew she was lying.

"I always look like I'm lying because I'm nervous because I've been in prison," she said. "Once a person has been in prison, the police officers . . ."

Shaking his head, Cabrera said, "No, no," and Puente broke in sharply, "Yes, it is."

She tried to persuade him of her good intentions, "I want to get off parole. I've had a good record." She splayed her hands out, her white, flabby arms, before the skeptical detective. "I've got nothing to hide. I don't want to go back to prison. I'm an old lady. I'm trying to get off parole. I'm trying to get my life together."

But Cabrera went right back to saying Bert was dead and more bodies were buried with him in the yard.

Puente tried indignation. "Well, I didn't put them there. I couldn't drag a body anyplace. My health's bad. I have a bad heart and I can't lift anything very heavy."

Cabrera wanted her to take a lie detector test. She said she was too nervous, but she'd take one Monday.

She would be long gone by Monday.

Puente showed Cabrera a little diagram of a trench he knew about that had been dug in February. She drew more and said the trench was for a sewer line she was looking for, and it went down a foot and a half and traveled straight for four feet. It was not a grave, she told Cabrera. Then he asked about another sewer line she'd had dug that summer by parolees from a halfway house. It was near the little trees where the body had just been found. Puente said she had dug up the whole backyard unsuccessfully searching for that sewer line. She was not digging graves.

"What about the lime we found? There was lime all around the body," Cabrera asked, jotting down notes.

"The people at Lumberjack told me lime would soften the dirt for my plants. I don't know how it got around any body."

But, she knew they were all lies. The police would dig them all up, Leona Carpenter, Dorothy Miller, James Gallop, Betty Palmer, Vera Martin, and of course, Bert Montoya. He was buried with the rest of them in the backyard.

When the police got under the toolshed, they would find Ben Fink, too. And there were others Puente's lies would not conceal for much longer.

She got to Stockton about 1:00 P.M. Saturday and told the cabbie to take her to the Greyhound bus terminal. She tipped him, went inside, and bought a ticket on the next bus, leaving at 2:00 for Los Angeles. Puente sat down among the farmworkers and their families, a spark of color and style, standing out vividly.

The bus ride south, down the long valley of California and into the thicket of people around Los Angeles, took over seven hours. Puente kept to herself, as people slept or talked around her. She had a brother and sister in the city, but she wasn't going to contact them. One of her two children, given up shortly after birth, lived in nearby South Pasadena, but Puente decided to stay away from her, too.

Around 10:00 P.M. the bus pulled into the Greyhound terminal in Hollywood. It was rowdy and seedy on a

Saturday night, and Puente quickly checked into a nearby hotel for the night.

Early Sunday morning she took a cab to the Royal Viking Motel on Alvarado. The rents were cheap, Hispanics from many countries lived in the neighborhood, along with many people on government assistance. It was the big city equivalent of Alkali Flat, a place where Puente felt comfortable and could move around confidently.

She gave her name to the front desk clerk as Dorothy Johansson. It was a name she had used before and she had once been married to a man named Johansson. She got a room across from the manager's office, number 31. Puente carefully prepaid for two nights, taking her into Monday.

Once in her room, she got out of her heavy red coat and tight shoes. For the first time since Friday morning she could really rest. She had escaped.

A little later the maid came and asked if she needed anything. Puente only opened the door a crack, smiled, and said, "Just towels, that's all," taking them from the maid. No one else was allowed in the room while she occupied it.

Near twilight on Sunday she felt hungry, got dressed again in the red coat and walked down the street, past a whitewashed apartment building and tall palm trees, to the T.G. Express restaurant which sold "Thai Chinese Food." It was part of the Royal Viking. Puente ordered a beer, drank it and some soup, then got another beer and chop suey in a plastic tray to take back to her motel room. As she walked the short distance, she passed newspaper vending machines. The Sunday *Los Angeles Times* shouted in headlines: "Two Bodies Unearthed at Boarding Home, Manager Sought".

Dorothea Puente walked quietly back to her room, locked the door, and ate her dinner. She had gotten away from Sacramento, but she was not safe. She had to plan what to do next, how to get money and shelter from the police.

5

By Sunday evening Sacramento was in an uproar. The prime suspect in a widening murder investigation had been helped to escape by the police. And the number of bodies found in the yard at 1426 F Street had risen to five. Each body was like the others, wrapped in blankets, secured with rope and duct tape. All appeared to be old or elderly men and women.

While both Cabrera and Terry Brown continued to dig at 1426 F, they were also detailed to compile lists of missing people around Alkali Flat and past tenants of Dorothea Puente. The body count might go on and on.

Each time another body was brought up, the crowd along the street surged toward the barricades for a better look. Lieutenant Joe Enloe held impromptu press conferences; swarms of cameras and microphones shoved at him in the chill drizzle. "We're getting scared now," he said after the third body was found Sunday. He had already given reporters a description of the first body found Friday: "It's the entire skeletal remains of a gray-haired, rather petite elderly

38

female." It was buried only three feet down and a scant hundred feet from the curb of F Street. An early estimate from the anthropologist and coroner was that this unidentified victim had been buried since April.

By now, Enloe was also briefing reporters about Puente's criminal background. In 1982 she had gone to prison for giving drugs to people, robbing them, forging their checks. He told the reporters that none of the bodies showed any sign of violence. "We don't expect that was the case."

The questions that would persist through the case had already been raised: How did these people die? Did Puente kill them? Did she have help? Did she have help burying them? The police thought she had an accomplice, "probably male." That was just a guess.

Sprinkled among the crowd were friends of Dorothea Puente, too. A stocky, dark-haired cabdriver named Patty Casey watched the bodies and machinery at 1426 F Street with horror and fear. She and Puente had become friends during the many cab trips Puente took to buy cement for "home improvements" or carpeting for a room Puente said was cursed. People died in the room, blood flowing from them and staining the old carpet.

"God, I love that person," Casey said of Puente. "I'm sorry my friend might have done something so horrible."

By Sunday, the Sacramento County District Attorney's Office had been on the case for two days. Cabrera had called frequently, seeking legal advice about exactly what he could do as the investigation developed.

His contact was Tim Frawley, one of the deputies in Major Crimes and the normal on-call lawyer that week. It was sheer coincidence that Frawley had filed the original cases against Puente in 1982. When Cabrera first called him, he didn't even remember Puente.

Frawley was athletic, diligent, with a reputation among lawyers and judges for fairness. His first act had been to counsel Cabrera that Puente should not be arrested Friday. There was too little evidence pointing directly at her.

Frawley's next step was to start a search warrant for 1426 F Street. That was the best way to preserve any evidence Cabrera or other cops found from future legal attack.

On Saturday Frawley said Puente could be arrested for Bert Montoya's murder, even if neither of the two bodies found at that point matched him. The problem, as Cabrera ruefully admitted, was that Puente was gone by then.

So the DA and cops turned to Puente's closest associate. Frawley took Cabrera's information about McCauley and around noon Sunday, decided to arrest the shaking, watery-eyed tenant of F Street. McCauley had lied to the police about when the backyard concrete had been poured, and denied getting a call from Puente after she left 1426 F Street Saturday. Frawley instructed Cabrera to arrest Mervin John McCauley as an accessory to murder: he might say something about Puente's location. Frawley wasn't overly optimistic, though.

Cabrera then escorted the thin, blue-jacketed McCauley down the porch steps at 1426 F, holding him up a little. The crowd murmured at the sight. All Enloe said publicly was, "He was a confidant of hers. But we do not believe he was involved in the hands-on work involving the bodies." Frail, trembling, old McCauley couldn't have lugged any bodies anywhere, that was obvious. But it was equally obvious someone had.

By late Sunday the removal of soil and concrete from the L-shaped backyard was so complete that two dump trucks had joined the crowded collection of police cars, coroner's vans, and TV trucks in the street. The spectacle of lights, people, sirens, cameras, was bigger than Cabrera or any of the other cops could recall.

One man in the crowd shivered watching a tractor load dirt and uprooted little fruit trees into the dump trucks. He had almost rented a room from Puente. He was on Social Security disability, which interested her greatly. But he stayed away finally because the rumors around Alkali Flat were that she could be very rough. Tenants ate when she said, got their medicine when she directed, were punched, slapped, or screamed at if they crossed her.

The load of dirt fell into one of the dump trucks. "I'm glad it wasn't me," the man said.

Frawley worked at his office on Saturday and Sunday, reviewing the reports that were starting to come in, fielding calls from the police working at F Street or their supervisors downtown. The blocky beige DA's office had no heat on weekends, so it was chillier than usual.

He was also reaching out to people involved with Puente both in the present and the past. He spoke several times with John O'Mara, his supervisor in Major Crimes, about the course to take in getting the search warrant together quickly. O'Mara, a bluff, sometimes acerbic man with a beard, had also coincidentally been Major Crimes supervisor in 1982 when information came to him that Dorothea Puente might have murdered Ruth Munroe. For various reasons, he had concluded then that there was not enough evidence to go forward against Puente at that time and the Munroe murder had remained uncharged.

Both Frawley and O'Mara agreed on Sunday night that McCauley, now glumly sitting in the county jail, was not going to say anything harmful to himself or Puente. The case against him was brittle and he probably couldn't be held long in custody, either. It was just another of the frustrating realities Sunday night, with more bodies probably buried at 1426 F Street and Puente on the run.

It was decided to charge Puente with Bert Montoya's murder. No one held out any hope, given the developments of the last twenty-four hours, that he was alive.

Sunday night, Frawley called me. He had finally remembered Puente from 1982, when he had sent her crimes to me for prosecution. Now he wanted to know if I recalled anything from her 1982 crime spree that might help.

After six years, there wasn't much I could do for him. I felt shame that Puente had gone to prison in 1982, gotten out in

1985, and instantly returned to the scene of her crimes, picking up where she left off, with murder.

Frawley and I agreed to meet Monday morning at the DA's office.

On Monday, November 14, Frawley, O'Mara, and I took a strange, spur-of-the-moment walk from the DA's office to 1426 F Street under a suddenly blue sky, the ground still wet, the air sharp.

We had all known about Dorothea Puente since 1982, and we were going to the site of the murders she had committed.

The carnival look of the 1400 block had grown worse with good weather, and cops stood in front of the iron fence at 1426, while others tried to keep the crowd across the street orderly.

O'Mara was sour about the presence of so many TV cameras, several reporters recognizing him, so we hurriedly ducked past the police into the yard.

Joe Enloe, still in his shapeless white raincoat, called out teasingly to Frawley, "We have enough PC yet, Tim?" Frawley's caution on Friday not to arrest Puente without sufficient probable cause still rankled the police. The sixth body had just been found.

It was impossible, seeing the technicians, the activity, the crowd, not to realize something had gone very wrong. If Puente had been stopped in 1982, none of this would have happened. I had known Frawley since law school and later when we worked together at the DA's office. He, too, was unhappy that she so quickly and easily started killing again after prison.

Enloe acted as tour guide for us. The L-shaped yard was reduced to mud and packed ground, all flowers and grass stripped away. It looked like a battlefield. Men and women worked at holes, almost bumping into each other. The saddest site was a board near the center of the yard on which lay a red-cloth wrapped figure, the latest victim unearthed.

A detective wanted to know if we'd like to get in on the lottery. There was betting on how many bodies would be found. The highest estimate was fifteen. Frawley said a psychic announced on Sunday that Puente had buried a dozen people.

We passed the red-blanket wrapped body on the board, waiting to be carried out to the coroner's van, to the noisy notice of the crowd. It was apparently the body of another small woman, her shroud dusted with white lime, like sugar on a pastry. It was immensely sad seeing the body, buried like the garbage McCauley had warned Cabrera about.

Enloe was brisk as a guide. He pointed at the Berkeley anthropologist, down on his knees with three other people, beside another gravesite. "He sees all kinds of stuff," Enloe said of the blue-overalled man. "He found ground-down cigarette butts in three graves, a pack of cigarettes in one. We would've missed that."

O'Mara and I noticed a man standing under what had been the small side porch, now torn apart. It was the county coroner, in a neat pearl gray suit, talking to a cop. O'Mara was irritated that the notoriety of the Puente case was making officials feel the need to show themselves, as if they were finally doing something about Puente. "Fifty people all hanging around with nothing to do," O'Mara said.

We stopped with Enloe at the next door neighbor's yard, beyond a rickety wooden fence. A loose German shepherd barked and tried to reach us over the fence. "See, this house wasn't here two years ago," Enloe said. "It was just moved here. Look here," he pointed at a depression in the yard a few feet away. "We got one place already where she used to come out and dig here in the garden all the time."

"What is it?" Frawley pointed at the depression.

"Another body," Enloe said decisively.

It was not, though, only another false lead.

We stayed for some time, asking questions, the bustle of the diggers and machines going on around us. Finally Frawley and O'Mara had seen enough. But genial Enloe wanted us to see one more thing. He motioned toward the dry, unweeded grass of the next door lot. "This is where we found the teeth." He pointed upward to a second-story window in 1426. "That's her bedroom. We figure she threw the teeth out when she thought we were going to search the house Friday. We got one body without any teeth."

"What would she do with teeth?" Frawley asked.

"Hard to ID someone without dental work. It's going to be hard to ID these bodies anyway. They're in bad shape." Enloe's broad face broke into a grin. He knew Puente's past record now. "Besides, some of them were gold teeth."

That made perfect sense.

We left, passing the backhoe busily starting to churn up the tiny front yard, where the shrine to St. Francis had stood, and where the seventh and last body would be found on Monday morning. The stone birdbath and stone squirrels that had led to the shrine were dumped to one side.

So we were all back in the Puente case after so many years. We didn't talk about what had gone wrong. There was too much for Frawley and O'Mara to do. No one knew where Puente was or what she was up to, and the case was getting hotter by the hour.

6

FOR TWO DAYS, PUENTE HAD BEEN STAYING AS HIDDEN AS possible in room 31. She watched TV or rested, the motel room curtains drawn. She took towels from the maid and kept her out.

At night, wearing her purple pumps and red coat, Puente went only as far as the T.G. Express restaurant. She added barbecue pork to her menu of chop suey and beer. Then she hurried back to her room. She read the local newspapers and learned that McCauley was in jail, and she herself was reported in cities from Mexico to Nevada.

The only human contact she had had was with the night clerk at the restaurant, who found the old woman with white hair very gracious and pleasant, quite out of place on Alvarado with its dubious businesses, garish signs, and declining apartments.

But Puente was growing restless and fretful. The police were all over the map now looking for her; the knock on the door could come at any time. And her money was slowly and inexorably dribbling away.

She had to find a safe haven, and she had to get more money very soon.

She drank her beer and ate chop suey and planned, as she had planned for years, how to provide for herself.

On Monday night in Sacramento, Cabrera and other detectives, with a video camera and still photographers, used Frawley's just signed search warrant to thoroughly take 1426 F Street apart for evidence.

Cabrera, Brown, and the others divided the house up by rooms. Cabrera took Puente's bedroom. It was crowded, the bed filling half of it, pushed near the dresser-bureau, itself crowded with perfume bottles, cosmetics, and pictures. Puente had enough clothes, expensive but anachronistic dresses in styles decades old, shoes, to make herself appear rich.

On the bed he saw the plush, heavy bedclothes, a blue stylish handbag tossed on it, a sign of Puente's hasty departure on Saturday. The bookshelves filled with paperback westerns, lurid romances, and mysteries made Cabrera wonder if Puente arrogantly believed she had read enough to trick the police. She had, of course, been very successful at doing just that.

From the bedroom window, Cabrera looked down on the dark, nighttime ruin of the backyard. Three people had been buried almost beneath that window. All of the bodies, in fact, had been under some marker—a toolshed, a fruit tree, a commode, a driveway, a shrine—whether to remind Puente where a body was buried or gloat over a kill, Cabrera never learned.

He quickly began finding pill bottles all around the bedroom, many for the tranquilizer Dalmane. It seemed to be everywhere. He went through each drawer of the bureau, hunting specifically for the drug. It was already clear that none of the victims at F Street had died by violence, although the headless body in the front yard might change that fact. Cabrera himself suspected the dead woman in the front yard had been mutilated after death to hide her identity.

It made very good sense, given Puente's past criminal history of drugging people in order to steal from them, to look for something that might render victims unconscious, or, in large amounts, kill them.

Cabrera was on to a solid lead. In the back of one drawer he found Dalmane capsules. Intrigued, he upended the wastebasket, sorting through the tissues, papers, trash. He was delighted to find fifteen empty Dalmane capsules. Someone had opened the capsules to pour the tranquilizer out, probably so that whoever was taking the drug wouldn't know it.

All of the evidence went into plastic bags or manila envelopes with the detectives' names and badge numbers on them and was recorded on the search warrant. Even if Puente wasn't found for years, the Homicide detectives wanted to maintain a clear, legally perfect chain of evidence for use in a trial.

No one wanted to even think about the possibility Puente was gone for good.

Cabrera and the other detectives turned their attention next to the "cursed" room Puente claimed existed near the kitchen. The investigation had revealed that she told tenants the foul smell coming from the room some months earlier was from a broken sewer line. She had shampooed the carpet many times to get rid of the odor, given up, and bought new carpet.

There was not much to see in the small room. Cabrera noted a bed covered with a quilt, more shelves of paperbacks, mops, and brooms. But something did smell peculiar. With another detective, Cabrera moved the bed, then some of the mops and brooms. The new blue carpet looked all right. Then they pulled it up. Both men coughed at the stink.

The second, original carpet had a large bloodstain on it and the mingled smell of bleach and blood was powerful.

This had nothing to do with Bert Montoya, however. Cabrera's training and the investigation told him that a decomposing body had lain in the room, leaking into the carpet, and Puente had not been prepared for that. Another missing tenant, Ben Fink, had gotten angrily drunk one night months before, something Puente hated. After trying to bully him into being quiet, she told the other tenants she would take "Ben upstairs and make him better." They saw her lead the swearing, feisty little man to her room, and then he was never seen again. She told the tenants Fink had left during the night.

Several days later, one tenant noticed what he described as "the smell of death" from the room near the kitchen.

Cabrera was certain Puente had left Fink's body in the room until she could decide what to do with it. It looked as though his body had been rolled up in the original carpet at some point. The carpets were torn up by the detectives, and the sound of wood being pried, slamming drawers, echoed through the house. It was a thorough, professional search, because Cabrera and the others knew that everything they did, in light of Puente's escape, was going to be scrutinized closely.

Frawley came by, checking on the search. Cabrera showed him a handwritten manuscript from Puente's bedroom, a Western novel. Puente told people she was a writer, along with her many other stories.

The detectives collected photographs from bookshelves and drawers. There were family shots of her "nephew" Ricardo Odorica and his children. Cabrera, Frawley, and the others looked with greater interest at pictures of Puente —younger, stout, wearing scarves and jewels, her white-blond hair done up in a stiff, obsolete hairdo from the 1940s—with famous people. Puente was standing with George Deukmejian, California's Attorney General, then Governor. She was photographed with Sacramento's Catholic bishop, a judge in his chambers, Representative Robert

Matsui, a leader in Congress. In some photos she was being given awards or plaques for work in the Hispanic community. She looked like a wealthy matron doing good works. All of the pictures had been taken within the last ten years.

She was a woman of contradictions and mystery, who could kill on charm, mix with the powerful and important or spend her days with the lowest members of the community.

Before they left the house around midnight, Cabrera and the detectives located prescriptions for Dalmane in Puente's name, and strange things like a driver's license with the name Betty Palmer and Puente's photo on it. There were letters in a dining room sewing cabinet to Vera Martin, bank deposit slips for Leona Carpenter.

Then, in a large envelope addressed to "Dr. Dorothea Puente," they discovered material to help identify the seven bodies. There was a medical ID for Bert Montoya in the envelope, along with a bank statement for Puente and Montoya, and another health card for Leona Carpenter. Dorothea Puente had wanted to keep this special information separate, apparently in case she needed to produce identification for people no longer able to identify themselves. In order to continue to get Social Security checks, or use a dead man's health benefits, Puente had to lay her hands on just the right documents. The envelope also held Veteran's Assistance papers for Dorothy Miller, Supplementary Security Income material for James Gallop, more letters to Vera Martin, letters to Ben Fink, his health card, and a medical card for Betty Palmer. The large envelope, clearly, had been hidden in the sewing cabinet drawer.

Cabrera was puzzled by several additional photos found of a smiling white-haired man with glasses. There were many names and faces to put to Puente's victims, and when the detectives left 1426 F Street Monday night, November 14, they were sure they had made a good start. But no one knew who the smiling man was that night.

A rookie cop, flashlight in hand for company, was left to guard the strange house. Floodlights blazed against it on the bitter cold November night, and the curious cars slowing down to look at the empty graves finally stopped coming and the street was silent.

7

ON TUESDAY, IF PUENTE HAD ANY IDEA OF THE FUROR SHE had stirred throughout the country, she was undoubtedly pleased. She always liked attention.

From Sacramento to Washington, agencies started investigations of their behavior in her case. The Department of Health Services in Sacramento ordered an investigation of how Puente, an ex-convict on federal parole too, could get medical assistance for her tenants and their Social Security checks every month. The Social Security Administration wanted to know that as well.

The DA was busy defending the police decision not to arrest Puente on Friday and the fact they had let her walk away on Saturday. John McCauley was quietly released from jail for lack of evidence and went into hiding from the reporters and cameras searching for him.

As for Sacramento Chief of Police John Kearns, he was in Los Angeles attending a conference of police chiefs and was spared the public criticism that his department was enduring. He refused his captains' repeated pleas to hurry back to Sacramento to defend the beleaguered department himself.

Joe Enloe was replaced as police spokesman on the case. It was a cosmetic change to show the department was sobering up after the giddiness of the first few days of international attention. News reports of the crimes had appeared in Europe and Australia.

To appease the public, the new police spokesman gruffly said that "every square inch of the yard" at 1426 F Street had been dug up. As he spoke, furniture, chairs, sofas, a mattress, desks, cans, filled boxes, were hefted from the house and dumped into trucks. Only Puente's large liquor supply, mostly vodka, in her bedroom and kitchen, was left untouched. There was no sign of any bodies inside 1426 F Street.

Nor did it appear that any more bodies would be found in the yard. The crowds, though, ever hopeful, stayed vigilant in front of the house through the next few days.

By the end of Tuesday, in fact, all digging had stopped. There had been a question whether Puente might have buried bodies at another boardinghouse she had run at 2100 F Street. It was a large, spacious house now owned by the family who lived in it. A new patio had been poured after Puente left, and the police were reluctant to tear it up. Metal probing, though, showed no sign of hidden graves.

The only other issue was the vacant lot across the street from 1426 F. A woman, perhaps looking like Puente, had been seen digging there in the recent past. Cabrera wanted to search the lot, primarily for the missing head, hands, and lower legs of the seventh body. O'Mara told the cops to do so quickly to avoid a rush of crowds and reporters. Digging aimlessly around the Alkali Flat neighborhood would only make everyone, police and DA, look more foolish. Sacramento was already in a state of wild excitement about the buried bodies.

Although Cabrera was convinced a neat package of body parts was buried in the lot, a police captain declared he was "putting an end to this media circus" and prohibited any digging in the lot.

The police and DA, with the piles of furniture, photos, drugs, had a monstrous puzzle to sort through anyway without going after evidence that might not contribute much to proving Puente's guilt.

That, anyway, was the thinking on Tuesday.

The FBI had come into the manhunt because Puente was supposed to have crossed state lines. The Sacramento police had roused their Las Vegas colleagues to watch the airport for her.

But on Wednesday, November 16, 1988, Dorothea Puente was still in Los Angeles and restless enough to venture out during the daylight. It was cool enough so she needed her red wool coat, but not damp, and she left her umbrella in room 31 at the Royal Viking.

It was good to get out of the room. Without maid service the empty chop suey cartons, beer bottles, newspapers were stacking up. She made the bed by throwing the covers over it. The air was thick.

She walked down slightly uneven sidewalks, buses rumbling by, through a welter of voices in Spanish, Korean, and English. It was a city Puente had known twenty years earlier when she was working more or less consistently as a prostitute. On Wednesday she was on the prowl again.

In her purple pumps she walked about a mile and a half from the motel, past salesmen watching for customers from doorways, cheap electronic stores, bus stops. Anyone who saw her could have called the police.

It might have been that awakening fear of discovery that made Puente turn at mid-afternoon into a bar, the Monte Carlo I, a neighborhood joint very much like her old Joe's Corner.

Inside, the room was dim, the bar horseshoe-shaped. A woman sitting at the far end watched Puente, then went back to drinking.

Puente sat down on a stool and ordered vodka and orange juice. There was a man at the bar, older, with glasses, with a worn and tired look that echoed Mervin John McCauley or several others she knew. He was sitting alone, midweek, midafternoon, drinking in a bar.

She did not start the conversation. The man politely said to her, "The heat from the refrigerator motor comes right out where you're sitting."

She thanked him, ordered another screwdriver, and picked up her purse and drink and moved to a barstool near him. She told him her name was Donna Johansson.

She asked him his name. He said he was Charles Willgues, he was a retired carpenter. He lived alone in an apartment about two blocks away on West 2nd Street. He had just bought a glass cutter and thought that a beer would taste good.

Willgues was impressed by the woman's bearing, her intelligence, and fashionable appearance. He talked easily to her, listened as she listed her tribulations.

Puente was, by turns, charming and put upon. As she drank she told Willgues that her shoes needed work. She turned her leg to him. She had done a lot of walking in the last few days. Her husband had died a month ago, and she had come south from Sacramento on Monday. She wanted to put her grief behind her, get a job, start a new life in a new city.

Willgues nodded. He knew all about grieving and struggling with hope.

But, Puente went on, my luck's been terrible since I got to Los Angeles. "I can't find work. I'm all alone. Everybody's been taking advantage of me since I got here."

She warmed to the tale. "Why, the cabdriver who brought me from the bus station was a crook. Do you know the Royal Viking Motel on Third and Alvarado?"

"Sure I do," Willgues said.

"Well, that cabdriver who took me there drove away with four of my suitcases. I've only got an overnight bag left. My shoes are all worn down, I've been walking so long trying to find a good place to stay."

Willgues offered to have her shoes fixed. There was a repair store nearby. Puente thanked him, fished out three dollars from her purse, and sat quietly drinking while he took her shoes.

It wasn't long before Willgues came back. Smiling gratefully, Puente slipped her purple pumps on again. Willgues had another beer. She had another screwdriver.

"How do you support yourself? Since you're retired?" she asked.

Willgues said he was sick and got Social Security. He had arthritis and emphysema and had suffered two strokes. He got a monthly check for $576.

"You could easily get $680!" she said quickly. "I can show you how to do it." She slipped in information about assistance payments and social service agencies to show her expertise.

They had been together about an hour and a half, and the November afternoon was softening outside the bar.

Puente put a proposition to Willgues, who plainly enjoyed her company. "We're two lonely people in a big city. I've got no one left, and you don't either. I hate spending holidays alone. Thanksgiving's coming up, and you should be with someone on Thanksgiving."

Willgues nodded. "I suppose so. I suppose it's better."

"I'm a very good cook. Why don't I make Thanksgiving dinner for you at your apartment?"

"Well, maybe. I don't know."

"Why don't we share an apartment? I can make life easier for you, straighten out your Social Security. Together life would be a lot easier for us both."

Willgues wasn't instantly persuaded. He had lived alone for years. "I've got enough to think about with myself," he said. "I don't want to take on somebody else." He did say he'd think about it.

"How about tomorrow?" Puente asked. "How about getting together again Thursday?"

Willgues agreed. They could go shopping for new clothes to replace the stolen ones. They could go out in the morning.

He gave her one of his business cards, *"Chuck the Handyman,"* and in large, confident strokes, Puente wrote on the back, "Donna Johansson, #31, 2025 3rd." Willgues added her phone number and the name of the motel underneath.

He called a cab for her because it seemed wrong to wear down her only good shoes right after they were repaired. Puente asked Willgues to buy her two dinners at a nearby fast-food chicken restaurant. She wanted to take them back to the motel and eat one later rather than go out on the dangerous city streets after 5:00 P.M.

"No wings, please," she said with a smile, handing Willgues twenty dollars for the dinners.

He got the dinners and had them ready for her by the time the cab showed up. "Remember our date tomorrow," Puente said.

"I'll call you first," Willgues agreed.

It was after four when Puente, balancing her hot dinners, slipped past the manager's office at the Royal Viking, into her room and locked the door.

It had been a profitable afternoon. She had a change of menu for dinner, a place to stay until Thursday, the prospect of new lodgings, and a man with health problems and Social Security benefits as a fresh companion.

Charles Willgues did not stay at the Monte Carlo I much longer after Donna Johansson left in the cab. He walked two blocks back to his apartment, thinking about her. He was puzzled. The bar was dim, but he'd had a good look at her.

He had a strange feeling he'd seen her face somewhere before.

But where? Why did she seem so familiar?

8

A GLOOMY, DROOPY-EYED JOHN KEARNS, SACRAMENTO'S CHIEF of Police, finally faced the massed cameras and rowdy reporters in the small makeshift press room. He had come back to Sacramento and landed in the middle of controversy about his own competence and his department's professionalism.

He promptly blamed Cabrera and others for letting Puente get away. "The Sacramento Police Department made an error. As a result, we lost a suspect."

The reporters asked blunt, unpleasant questions about why Kearns had stayed in Los Angeles, why the investigation looked so amateurish.

"She should have been followed. There aren't any excuses, as far as I'm concerned, why the suspect wasn't kept under surveillance."

He had a ready explanation, based on Puente's grandmotherly exterior and pliant behavior. "She'd been talked to by detectives and established a dialogue, and I feel that

57

what occurred was that we possibly became too familiar with the suspect and too trusting."

Homicide detectives are not supposed to be lulled into trusting a suspect.

Kearns was angry, sharp, defensive for the entire press conference. His words shook the department because the Chief was not supporting his detectives, but hanging them out as problems to be fixed.

Cabrera, Brown, Enloe, and others were veterans of enough police department politics to recognize the sound of management closing ranks against them. No captain or supervisor or the Chief would be blamed for Puente's escape, her long murderous activities, or the anger if she was never caught.

At the Sacramento County Coroner's Office, a dour modern building looking like a suburban bank, connected to the Crime Lab, the third body dug up at F Street was taken from its wrappings, and laid out on a white metal table under bright white lights.

The third body had been chosen because it was a man and matched, roughly, the description of Bert Montoya.

Four people worked carefully over the body, talking calmly, noting down what they saw and did for use in court.

The body was wrapped in a green blanket that was sprinkled with lime and tied with string. At the head, giving it a comic appearance, the knot was tied in a bunch.

What struck the pathologists and technicians first were the almost obsessional number of inner wrappings around the body, fourteen in all, cloth, plastic, secured with duct tape, then a quilt, and more plastic. Finally, in a pathetic revelation, the man himself lay under the merciless lights. He weighed, now, about 128 pounds. He wore gray trousers, jockey shorts, striped socks and a white T-shirt and looked to be between 50 and 60 years old. What hair remained on his scalp was light brown and wispy. He had been buried in such a way that his arms were raised, elbows flexed, at the side of his head, as if warding off something.

He was grotesque, in advanced decomposition, swollen, discolored and dripping fluids. He did have a bit of sideburns and mustache left, but most had rotted off.

With his clothes cut off, bathed in white light, stared at, exposed completely, dirt brown, the man looked almost like a giant russet potato.

His fingers were cut off to use in developing any prints. Dropped into a bottle of formaldehyde, they would be sent to the California Department of Justice's Latent Fingerprint Section.

The pathologists carefully removed the vital organs, noting some liver enlargement and hardening of the arteries. Brain tissue was preserved, and blood specimens taken. From these it might be possible to detect the presence of any drugs. Drugs tended to collect in brain matter or remain in blood, but the body's severe decay, like that of the other six from 1426 F Street, would make the task of detection very complicated and uncertain. The man's brain, for example, had decayed considerably, leaving a residue that had collapsed against the rear of the skull in a puttylike mass.

From the examination of fingerprints, a 1984 mastoid operation matched by body number three at the autopsy, the coroner announced that this was indeed Alvaro "Bert" Montoya.

Bert's eighty-two-year old mother, living in New Orleans, was notified. Moise and Valentine took the expected but still shattering news with a combination of resignation and bitterness. They had known something was wrong with Dorothea Puente and yet Bert had been forced to go back to 1426 F Street when he tried to get away.

Who else, they wondered, of their lonely, sad clients, lay on metal trays in the coroner's office, waiting to be identified?

For them and the police and DA, the questions remained stark. What had killed Bert? Or the others?

And who, Cabrera wondered, was the smiling, white-haired man with glasses in the photo in Puente's dining room? Why had she kept the picture hidden?

Worse, for everyone seeking answers, would Dorothea Puente ever be found? Earlier that day, at his raucous, uncomfortable press conference, Chief Kearns had allowed himself one bit of sensational speculation. In answer to a question, Kearns had said, "If someone's going to kill seven people, why stop there?"

Around 9:00 P.M. Wednesday night, Puente got a phone call. The local newscasts had again featured her face, her alleged seven murders, the vast law enforcement army seeking her across America.

It was Charles Willgues on the phone. He wanted to see how she was doing and whether they were still going out in the morning.

Puente said yes, they were, she had eaten the dinner he got her, and she'd be staying in that night.

When she hung up after Willgues's call, Puente was full and drowsy after a long day. She had been drinking screwdrivers and beer, eaten two chicken dinners. Her future security was shaping up. She could look forward to Thursday and her next meeting with Chuck the handyman who was apparently very interested.

PART 2

The mass murderer lies to himself.

William Bolitho,
Murder for Profit

9

WHO WAS DOROTHEA PUENTE AND WHERE HAD SHE COME FROM? Was there something in her early life, however much it was like that of millions of other people who never killed anyone, that set her toward murder?

There are mysteries around Puente, but some central answers, too.

The basic truth about her is that she always sought control. Her essential appetite was to control the people and situations around her. From an early age she was a practiced liar, graduating to minor crimes, then more serious ones, and finally murder. But the basic purpose of every criminal act was to control the world she lived in.

So Puente invented a glamorous past for herself, called herself a lawyer or doctor, and claimed a love affair with the Shah of Iran and a movie career. She was a smart, resourceful, and very attractive woman for much of her life, but also a very disturbed one.

In 1985, as she was about to be released back to Sacramento after serving time in prison for drugging, robbery, and forgery, a psychologist for the state Department of Corrections did an in-depth evaluation of the new parolee. He might have been describing Dorothea Montalvo Puente's entire life to that point:

> Montalvo appears to disassociate herself from any of the crimes for which she has been arrested and received time. She tends to minimize the importance of what she did or her responsibility for any of them [*sic*].
>
> It appears at this time that although Montalvo does not evidence any symptoms of psychosis—that is, hearing voices or having delusions of grandeur—that she is in fact, schizophrenic. . . .
>
> This woman is a disturbed woman who does not appear to have remorse or regret for what she has done, and who at least on two occasions has been involved with administering drugs and/or poison to unwitting victims. She is to be considered dangerous, and her living environment and/or employment should be closely monitored.

Puente told the psychologist she loved children and would enjoy being a baby-sitter, but the psychologist wisely concluded that she should be kept away from children and the elderly; vulnerable people were at grave risk when Puente was near them.

Yet this dangerous woman had shown great kindness and lavished attention on a number of orphaned or poor Mexican girls, helped sick people around Alkali Flat, and genuinely contributed to Hispanic community groups, even though she wasn't Hispanic.

But the anomaly evaporates in light of Puente's lifelong yearning for attention and control. As a rough boardinghouse mistress or civic benefactress, she achieved the control and respect she desperately coveted.

It was the same hunger that set her up for years as a

prostitute, where, paradoxically, her degree of control over others may have been the greatest.

The only problem for Puente as a great community leader and charitable donor was that her dream life required real money. She first got money through theft and forgery, then murder.

Why did Puente turn to murder? Her adulthood was cleft by two great calamities. In 1978 she lost her status as a well-off civic leader when she was convicted on federal forgery charges. This loss of position devastated her. When she was faced again, in 1982, with actually going to prison and losing her self-created role as a community figure, she first resorted to murder, killing Ruth Munroe in order to get quick money to flee the country.

After she got out of prison in 1985, Puente had no hesitation about killing again and again to protect her control, her dream image as a fashionable, important woman.

But where did the roots of murder lie? Killing for profit isn't predestined, yet in the mundane, sad details of Puente's unhappy childhood and later life, at least a fuller picture of this awful and driven woman exists.

"When I was 3 years old, I had to start picking cotton, potatoes, cucumbers, chilis, then fruits. I finally married when I was 18, he died after a few days."

So Puente began a letter to a judge in 1982, hoping to reduce her prison sentence. Like her life itself, Puente's letter mixes a little fact with much fiction in order to manipulate the observer. Her husband did not die nor was she married at 13. But her early years were hard and formative.

Born Dorothea Helen Gray on January 9, 1929 in Redlands, a moderately sized city in San Bernardino County, California, Puente was the sixth of seven children. She later claimed to be the youngest of eighteen brothers and sisters.

Her father was Jesse James Gray from Missouri. Gray

fought in World War I and was severely burned by mustard gas; as a result he developed tuberculosis. The war, his continuing illness and debility, left Gray deeply depressed, which he sometimes expressed by saying he wanted to kill himself. He let his children, including little Dorothea, know that he thought life was vicious, mean, and he was the object of unfair treatment.

Puente's mother was Trudy Mae Gates and had come from Oklahoma. She was tougher, physically and emotionally, than her husband. A small-faced, pretty woman, she had a rough, rebel nature from the start of the marriage.

Because the Depression left the sick, despondent man Gray with little opportunity, the whole family worked at jobs around Redlands, sometimes moving with crops. It was an unpleasant, cold life, the children often left to fend for themselves when their parents argued bitterly, or more frequently, drank heavily. Trudy particularly, drank and stayed away from her husband and children. The older children took care of the younger ones, and Puente was essentially raised by her older brothers and sisters.

She had learned an interesting trick before she was six or seven years old. By faking illness or fabricating complex fantasies about her importance, Puente escaped the drudgery and terrors of early childhood. During the times she spent in school, Puente was often chastised by her teachers for lying.

In 1935, Gray was in and out of hospitals for increasingly futile treatment of his TB. While he was gone, Trudy spent much of her time with a motorcycle gang. She would lock Dorothea and an older brother in a closet for days at a time when she left. On her return, she threw up, made other messes, and Dorothea was expected to clean up after her. Trudy spent time in county jail, too, for drunkenness, leaving her seven children without either parent at home.

But when Trudy was at home, she lectured Dorothea about helping other people and the need to be of service to others. "Mother once made me promise to feel sorry for alcoholics and to take care of drunks," Puente said later in life. It is obvious that raised in a household in a constant uproar, with a mother often drunk or in jail, Puente early on formed her mixed detestation of drunks and her desire to make them better.

The family moved to Los Angeles in late 1936, where Gray's health faded inexorably and Trudy's drunken sprees continued, as did her time in jail. Dorothea joined her mother, and the remaining children who had not been split up between other relatives or neighbors, in February 1937. The household was coming apart completely.

Gray had gone back into the hospital in December 1936, and his condition never improved. He died on March 29, 1937, after Dorothea had been reunited with him only for a month.

Left with several children to raise, Trudy moved them to San Dimas, a smaller city, dry and dusty at the end of 1937. Her drinking was steady and brutal for Dorothea and the remaining children. When this became apparent to teachers and others who saw the children, Trudy lost custody of Dorothea in early 1938. Nine years old, with a sad-eyed, pretty face, Dorothea entered an orphanage run by the Church of Christ in Ontario, California. Her endless lying and imaginative fantasies were remarked on by the staff who cared for the unhappy, abandoned little girl.

On December 27, 1938, Trudy was killed in a motorcycle accident and Dorothea, now a true orphan, was desolated. No amount of dreaming or hard work had succeeded in saving either her mother or her father, keeping her brothers and sisters together, or preventing her from being left with strangers in an orphanage.

But Dorothea was not merely a little girl with a wretched childhood. She was also highly intelligent and had hardened around her a carapace of self-sufficiency. If she could not save others or trust them to take care of her, she would have to do it herself.

Sent to live with a succession of near relatives or older brothers or sisters, Puente rarely spent more than a few months in any one place, living a nomadic, unsettled life.

She was in Napa at the age of thirteen, then dipped for one semester into school in Los Angeles at sixteen.

At sixteen, Dorothea was dark-haired and slim, with hard black eyes, an appraising attitude toward people. By her lies and actions, she was going to shape the world to her wishes rather than let the world buffet her further. Her beauty was a tool, able to bend people to do as she wished.

World War II found Dorothea no better off than she had been in the thirties, until in 1945 she was sent back to Los Angeles to live with an older sister and her husband. But Dorothea, now alive to the possibilities offered by her own attractiveness, ran away, heading north. She was perceived by another sister, many years later, as having changed forever. "Sometimes," Dorothea's sister said in 1988, "when people have a hard childhood, their own world is so hard, they make up a pretend one."

Dorothea ended up in Olympia, Washington, in the summer of 1945, as the war was ending. She had invented a name for herself—Sheri—and worked as a waitress in a milkshake parlor. She had also begun working, for the first time, as a prostitute.

Prostitution was a simple way to capitalize on her physical beauty, make up any story she liked about her identity, and control her customers, too. As a prostitute, for the first time in her life, she felt she had a form of power.

It is also possible that Trudy Gray had worked, at least some of the time, as a prostitute, and brought customers home while Jesse was away or in the hospital. Trudy ran with a motorcycle gang, had trouble holding a job, drank heavily, and needed money. It was a recipe for prostitution.

Dorothea never had any scruples about being a hooker and since she learned so many things, or transmuted them like the advice about helping drunks, from her mother, it is possible she picked up prostitution as well.

After working for several months as Sheri, Dorothea met a twenty-two year old soldier coming back from the Philippines. His name was Fred McFaul and he was about six years her senior. McFaul discovered Dorothea and a girl-

friend using a motel room as a trick pad. That did not
bother him. He found Dorothea wildly attractive and even
admired her ruthless desire to survive. She would do almost
anything, he realized. Years later from a hospital bed,
McFaul said, "She knew how to make a buck when she
wanted to."

No matter what her problems were, McFaul determined
to marry Dorothea and did so in November 1945 in Reno,
Nevada. Although she was still sixteen, Dorothea listed her
age as thirty on the marriage certificate and invented a
fuller, imaginary maiden name for herself, Sherriale A.
Riscile. The name puzzled her new husband, but he was
getting used to her constant confabulations, the endlessly
spun tales about her life, things she had done, the things she
planned to do. When they met strangers, around town or at
bars, McFaul marveled at his new bride's capacity to con
anyone. She could smile, chat, tell a tall tale, and in a few
minutes, convince anyone she had just recounted the honest
truth. She was a fashion model, an actress, royalty, anything
at all.

By 1945, having followed her mother's footsteps and
married a returning soldier, Dorothea McFaul started
drinking in earnest, and tried to start a family.

For the first two years of her marriage to McFaul,
Dorothea lived in the remote, dusty little town of
Gardnerville, Nevada. She had two daughters between 1946
and 1948, but couldn't stand to have either child around
her. She and McFaul quarreled with the same intensity and
bitterness as her parents had. The couple would not raise the
children, Dorothea hated the idea, and McFaul was unable
to prevent his strong-willed wife from doing as she pleased.

The first daughter was sent to live with relatives in
Sacramento. The second, in 1948, was put up for adoption.
Dorothea's second and last living child grew up as Linda
and spent years tracing her biological mother, anxious to
learn where she had come from.

The drinking and fights with McFaul, the strain of giving
her second child to strangers, sent Dorothea to Los Angeles

for about a month. She probably went back to prostitution to support herself. McFaul, even through the haze of their quarrels and many years, thought back on Dorothea in 1988 and said, "She was a good-looking female," with admiration.

After she went back to McFaul and the narrow life in Gardnerville, Dorothea miscarried, and it was this that apparently brought the marriage to a final end. McFaul had put up with her strange ideas, fancies, her lust for constant attention and compliments, and found that he could no longer trust her to tell him even the most basic truth. He left her in late 1948 and they later divorced.

For a woman with her difficulty maintaining a sense of self-importance and respect, McFaul's departure was a wounding blow. For the rest of her life, Dorothea Puente told everyone that her husband had died soon after they were married, sometimes as quickly as within two days.

She left Nevada and went back to California, heading for San Bernardino, another dry, dusty city in the southern part of the state, and near where she had been raised. Dorothea struggled through a succession of jobs, and at last embarked on the path of crimes that eventually took her to 1426 F Street and murder.

She began stealing checks in 1948 from a woman she had befriended. She used the checks to buy shoes, stockings, a hat, and purse. The next day she tried to buy $84.83 worth of shoes using a check drawn on the account of Sherriale A. Riscile, her imaginary name.

But Dorothea was not the practiced con artist she later became. Something in her nervous manner aroused the suspicion of the store manager and he refused the check. She hurried out and, almost in a panic, took a bus to the nearby city of Ontario.

But, by that time, the manager had alerted the police. They knew about the earlier forgeries and that Riscile was an alias. They were waiting when Dorothea arrived in Ontario and arrested her.

For the first time in her life, she was seen by a doctor. He was interested in her mental state, to see if she knew the nature of the charges and if she was mentally competent. Dorothea's lies to her woman friend and the store manager had apparently raised doubts about her emotional balance.

The county appointed doctor learned that the sometimes haughty, sometimes weeping young woman he talked to, had a "compelling need to buy clothes and re-establish her own self-esteem." It was a diagnosis repeated for forty years about her. She was not, the doctor told the court, "a true criminal," but really only "a situational offender." She would commit crimes only when opportunities presented themselves and she thought she could evade punishment.

Dorothea did not want to go to trial and expose her dream life to the rigors of cross-examination by a prosecutor or the judge. She worked out a plea bargain, as she would do again for forty years, and told the judge she was indeed guilty of two counts of felony forgery and one count of writing a fictitious check. She was sentenced to a year in county jail, based on the favorable report of the doctor, and actually served only four months.

In jail, faced with adult punishment at last, Dorothea's hardened self-sufficiency and survival instincts took over. She was respected by the other women for her brains, and her ability to get along with the guards. She begged or scrounged small favors, like candy and cigarettes, for herself and her friends.

When she was released, Dorothea moved north, having told her probation officer she lived in San Francisco. But in May 1950, only six months after her release, Dorothea disappeared. In Riverside County, which had jurisdiction over her probation, a judge issued a warrant for her arrest. While in jail, Dorothea had picked up useful knowledge about how the criminal justice system worked. Warrants for a routine small time forger would usually go to the bottom of a deep stack of other warrants for more serious crimes.

Dorothea was never arrested on the Riverside warrant. She changed her name again, kept moving, and even her relatives, the brothers and sisters she still wrote to, finally lost track of her. For a long time during the fifties, her family thought she was dead.

She was very much alive, though, and had probably returned to prostitution for easy money and to maintain her dream life. In 1952, Dorothea met and married Axel Johansson, who was as captivated by the smart, bustling, beautiful woman as Fred McFaul had been. He, too, was at first beguiled, then bewildered, then angry with her endless lies and stories.

Over the next few years the couple set up housekeeping in northern California in Sacramento or nearby cities. But Dorothea was restless and left for long periods, returning to Los Angeles, drifting around. When she did come back to Johansson, they fought about her absences and her being a hooker. Once again Dorothea was replicating her own home life with Jesse and Trudy.

But she was very much her own woman. She had learned a lot in jail, and while working as a hooker. By 1960, Dorothea had opened and run several brothels, sometimes employing several other women, or just herself and one other woman. She had far more business sense and fewer scruples than her mother ever did.

But boldness and brains, like luck, go only so far. In early 1960, Dorothea was once again the object of serious law enforcement interest.

The slim, lively young woman McFaul had married in 1946 had grown fat by 1960, still attractive, but over thirty years old, too. Dorothea was having considerable trouble working as a hooker, and no amount of makeup or carefully draped clothing could hide her diminishing sexual appeal.

It reached the point that she started brothels, acting primarily as the madam, only sometimes as a hooker. If Johansson protested, Dorothea still had her own money now and could keep away from him.

Her luck ran out in April 1960. The owner of a property on Fulton Avenue in Sacramento complained to the Sheriff's Department that what he thought was being rented as a bookkeeping service was actually a whorehouse. He was indignant and demanded something be done to stop it.

The phony bookkeeping service had a special telephone number for clients. The specialty of the house was a blow job for seven dollars and fifty cents.

Two deputy sheriffs staked out the address. They saw men coming in and out all day. The business, whatever it was, kept very regular hours, and closed promptly at 5:00 P.M.

Whoever was running the office had camouflaged it well and demonstrated they were clever. The sheriffs set up a sting to catch the operator in the act.

Two deputies dressed as truckers and rented a semitrailer and tractor. They coated twenty-five dollars in five-dollar bills with fluorescent powder as bait money. The deputies put powder on their hands, too.

They then went to a phone booth several miles from Fulton Avenue and used the special number to call the business. A woman answered and said they could come ahead. She would take care of them for the usual price— $7.50 apiece.

With backup squad cars nearby, the phony truckers drove their rig up to the Fulton Avenue address. The woman who met them at the door was in her early thirties, large built, with penetrating black eyes. She looked pretty in a fleshy way. She said her name was Teya Johansson, and she and her associate, Bonnie Lacoste, would happily service the two men.

Johansson told the deputies that she preferred giving blow jobs to customers, but would agree to a straight fuck if the men would use rubbers. Since there was only one bed, Lacoste would take the first trucker, and Johansson would give his friend some coffee while they waited. Johansson then reconsidered. She would only give a blow job after all.

She took fifteen dollars in fluorescently marked money from one of the deputies. He abruptly asked if her breasts were as big as they looked. Johansson smiled and said both men could fondle them, for free, if they liked. One deputy, to complete the sting, put his hand inside Johansson's dress and rubbed a breast, coating it with powder.

The two deputies followed Lacoste to the lone bed and watched her undress. As she raised her skirt, one deputy touched her legs and buttocks to mark her. Then a surprised Johansson and Lacoste were arrested for prostitution. The marked bait money was retrieved from an annoyed Johansson. Other evidence seized from the office included Johansson's trick appointment book, which listed regular customers at rates varying from seven dollars down to fifty cents.

Taken downtown, to the old county jail, a matron stripped both women. Johansson did not protest much. Using an ultraviolet light, the matron passed it over Johansson's naked body, the fluorescent powder glowing blue on her breast, back, and knee.

Dorothea Puente, using the false name Teya Johansson when talking to people face to face, had employed a different phony name when she called a month or two earlier from Los Angeles to rent the Fulton Avenue property. She had said she was going to be doing business in bookkeeping, mostly with men from Reno.

Puente had progressed very far from the simple motel room she used as a trick pad in 1945.

Still clinging to the false Teya Johansson name, Puente was charged finally with being in a house of ill repute, a misdemeanor. She had sidestepped the tougher charge of pimping and pandering by agreeing to plead guilty quickly. Like her 1948 forgery plea, Puente calculated that a quick plea, a lighter sentence, was better than risking cross-examination. She had a sophisticated sense of survival and what the criminal justice system could do to her.

Standing before the judge, looking puzzled, contrite, and motherly, Puente said she had been visiting a girlfriend when the deputies arrived. The judge didn't believe her and gave her ninety days in county jail.

She served her time without incident and continued to lie about the crime for thirty years. The actual arrest report, she knew, for a misdemeanor charge, would sink swiftly under the tide of new cases, so she could lie about it with impunity.

When she got out of jail, Puente went back to Axel Johansson, who must have been furious she had used part of her married name as a hooker. They went on fighting, Puente spending more time away from Johansson. The couple moved to Broderick, across the river from Sacramento, and lived there for three years. Puente held down a series of short-term jobs, a cook, a dishwasher, anything that came along, while buying clothes and make up constantly.

Finally, as McFaul had done before him, Johansson could not stand the mysterious absences of his wife, her erratic behavior, lies, drinking, scheming, and he sued for divorce in 1966.

This ended the first phase of Dorothea Puente's life. As the sixties and her second marriage came to a close, she had reckoned that prostitution was too small-time and risky for her. Nearly forty years old and growing quite fat, she turned to what became her life's occupation: looting health care businesses while elaborating a continuously imagined past of glamor, danger, and sacrifice.

10

Casting a predatory eye around the landscape of Sacramento in 1968, Dorothea Puente searched for the elderly, ill, or alcoholic. These were people left largely on the margins of society. But they still got bountiful state and federal checks, payments that could add up if one bundled these people all together in one place.

So Puente, who had learned how to operate a business profitably as a madam and hooker, opened the first of several unlicensed health care operations. She called it "The Samaritans," and it specialized in alcoholics, those people Trudy had made Dorothea promise to help. The bonus for Puente was that she could siphon off a little bit of money paid to each client and have a steady, untaxable income.

It was not a large operation. It was a testing ground for Puente, who learned as much from her mistakes as her successes. She supplemented "The Samaritans" income by hiring herself out as a twenty-four-hour-a-day caretaker and "nurse" for the elderly or invalided.

Working from a small building at the Capitol Guest

House on Alhambra Boulevard, Dorothea Johansson, as she now called herself, impressed every social worker who came by with her kindly manner and her concern for the alcoholics she tended. But Puente was also a stern woman, physically taking the drunks in hand, making them follow her schedule of meals and medication. She seemed, thought the social workers, so *motherly* in her compassion.

Puente learned to curry favor with city inspectors and social workers who came by. They could always find a sandwich waiting or a fresh piece of pie. She threw montly dinners for them, the whole groaning table of alcoholics and social workers, presided over by a beaming hostess.

In return for all of the attention she gave to others, Dorothea Puente only insisted that she be made payee for any money due her boarders and she have complete control over their checks.

If her public face was benign, orderly, secure, Puente in private was in disarray. She had ballooned up to nearly 200 pounds on a five-foot-eight-inch form, and she was drinking consistently and constantly in the evenings.

She began courting younger men, especially Hispanics. At the same time that she discovered the financial rewards of helping others, Puente also found that Hispanics were having a hard time in Sacramento. As a child in Redlands, working in the fields, she had known many migrant farmworkers. She had grown up around Mexicans and had learned some Spanish. People who were struggling to make a decent living, facing neglect, ostracized, were Puente's people. She could both comfort and master them, and these were always her intertwined compulsions.

She met and married a young Hispanic named Roberto José Puente who was twenty-one years old. She was thirty-nine. The disparity in their ages was matched by a collision of interests and attitudes. Dorothea dressed as fashionably as possible to hide her bulk, and acted like a great lady in public. She assumed she was important. Her new husband was boyish, without noticeable skill at any job.

The marriage was a flop from the start. The two, married in Reno, went back to Sacramento and fought every day. For perhaps the only time, Dorothea Puente misread another person's hopes and found herself on the short end of a bargain. She liked to use others as a meal ticket, not the other way around.

After only two bitter weeks, Roberto left her. She sued for divorce in 1969. Recounting this misadventure later, Dorothea said she had gotten married in Mexico after she visited relatives there. She claimed the man turned out to be a homosexual and they were married for seven years.

Shaken by the experience with Roberto, faltering in her motherly facade, Puente's business foundered. "The Samaritans" was $10,000 in debt, and she declared bankruptcy the same time as divorcing Roberto.

But she had picked up lessons in management, how many boarders she could handle, how to con outsiders, and most important, how to fully control the daily lives of her boarders and their money.

Within a short time, Dorothea was back in business as a board-and-care operator, in much larger quarters, with a more ambitious program.

She had leased a large three-story house at 21st and F Streets. It was a white, square house, Victorian and grand. It had sixteen small bedrooms and bathrooms and each room, like a hotel, contained a bed, television, and closets. Puente appropriated the entire third floor as her own residence, living literally over her boarders, as she would do again later at 1426 F.

In the ground floor she put the more affluent boarders who were on federal assistance. She relegated the poorest, county-assisted tenants to the basement in what one former tenant called "little cubicles with just curtains separating them."

But the change from the first operation was dramatic. Puente had up to two cooks permanently on staff, and on holidays she threw lavish parties for the social workers who sent people to her. Since the tenants Puente accepted did not require any specific medical or psychological program, she did not have to license the operation.

A cozy relationship developed between her and the social workers. Their perpetual problem was finding someone who would care for alcoholics, and Puente was happy to do so, provided she gained control over the assistance checks that came in.

It was a neat, nearly immaculate house. The dinner table was set carefully, gleaming with glassware. Even the refrigerator looked spotless. Keeping a place so clean with up to thirty problem drinkers going in and out was a tough job. Puente again impressed any official visitors with her loving care toward her tenants combined with a willingness to swear at them, push them, and compel them to take medication or follow her direction. She appeared to be the answer to a social worker's dream.

The only slight defect many people saw in her was a wild imagination. Not content to run a large alcoholic board-and-care facility well, Puente described herself variously as a medical doctor or a lawyer. She claimed acquaintance with famous actresses and public people, and said she had not only been on the Bataan Death March, but had survived the atomic bombing of Hiroshima as well.

Her official guests, eating a piece of pie she had offered, watching her sympathetically pat a troubled drunk, invariably decided to simply discount the lies and concentrate on her real accomplishments.

She had, though, gone a little further than many realized. In an office downstairs at 2100 F Street, Puente hung phony printed medical diplomas, bought medical equipment like blood pressure cuffs and syringes, and held herself out as "La Doctora." She gave what she claimed were vitamin shots to people who came to her informal clinic. Most were from the surrounding Hispanic neighborhood, and Puente provided an easy, friendly service.

One physician who stopped by 2100 F Street every month to examine the people living there found a willing assistant in Puente. She told him she was a qualified doctor, too, but he brushed that aside because he was impressed with her management of the business.

The two of them would set up in the kitchen, at the long table, the real doctor at one end, Puente at the other, and each tenant would come in, be checked over, then given a prescription if necessary. Puente acted as a stern lecturer, warning the tenants to take the medicine.

She could, though, blow her top. Sloppy drunks infuriated her.

If she saw a drunk in the house, Puente would rage instantly, her voice raised, cursing loudly and furiously. Her salty language startled people like the visiting physician, but he noticed that her rage had one salutary effect: the drunk never came around the house under the influence again.

Both the physician and other social service workers who dropped in unannounced to check on Puente's operation, conceded that she ran a tight, efficient business at 2100 F Street. Out of sight of these visitors, though, Puente had fights with tenants at night, especially when she had been drinking, and sometimes either she or the tenant ended up bloodied.

By the mid-seventies, Puente embarked on the two major enterprises of her life that transformed her into a woman of importance and compassion. She became a civic leader and she took struggling young Hispanics, usually women, under her wing.

"My impression was that she was a lonely person," Puente's lawyer in 1975, Don Dorfman, recalled. Busy with 2100 F Street, she nevertheless seemed to need something more to make her happy.

Puente solved her problem by devoting her considerable energy to making a mark in the downtown Hispanic community. She already served it as a "doctor," now she opened her purse as well.

Meeting a young Hispanic announcer without a job, Puente used her contacts in the community to launch his career on Spanish-language radio. She sponsored events, for medical aid or housing and donated money generously. No one cared where the money came from. The well-dressed, matronly Puente told anyone who asked that she was a rich woman who owned homes all over the world.

One of her pet charities was Hispanic performers, singers and musicians. Puente sponsored their entry into the United States, got them airtime on Spanish-language radio or television, acted almost as their agent.

By 1977, Puente's relentless promotion and good works had earned her a genuine place among Sacramento's Hispanics. She was always available to give money, make a phone call, or organize an event.

But she didn't limit her activities to charity. Puente also became a major contributor to political candidates. Her lawyer recalled one event when she bought an entire table at a fund raiser for Democratic Congressman Mervyn Dymally who was running to become California's Attorney General. Puente, dressed in her most elegant gown, her hair beautifully set and shining, sat at the table while the hundreds of politicians and other donors swirled around and stopped by to pay their respects.

She was always gracious, grand. Dymally came over, warmly embraced her and kissed her. They talked like old friends about his chances for election and the wonderful things he would do.

As people began dancing, California's Governor Jerry Brown, strolled over, also clasping the white-haired smiling Puente. He kissed her too, and, taking her hand, the two of them danced out among the important and wealthy campaign contributors. Puente had gone far on audacity and willpower. She had been in jail, worked for years as a hooker, and now danced at the pinnacle of California's political establishment.

Along the way, Puente did not limit herself to one political party. She also gave money lavishly to Republican candidates and posed for pictures with George Deukmejian, then Attorney General, later Governor. Bishop Francis Quinn praised her for her work in the Hispanic community and had his picture taken with her. Puente found herself the subject of glowing articles in Spanish-language newspapers published in Roseville and Sacramento.

But public honors and attention did not satisfy her. She hungered for something else, too. Her loneliness struck many people who saw her in 1976 and 1977. She frequently went to bars at night dressed in expensive fashions, made up with the most costly cosmetics, and struck up conversations with people she met, telling tall tales about her exploits. Some tales, though, were true.

If she didn't go out at night, and was sure that no one would drop in, Puente drank heavily and became that violent, obscenely cursing drunk that her mother had been and she herself detested.

Starting in the mid-seventies, Puente had begun accumulating hard-pressed young women, who found in her the mother they themselves did not have. One summer she took in twin sisters, both nine years old, and tutored them on how to be proper young ladies. She gave them motherly love as well, and protected them from their own abusive home lives. It was a story repeated a dozen times.

Puente's lawyer was surprised, at first, when she appeared in his office with children in tow, sad-eyed little girls in bright dresses.

"This is my stepdaughter," Puente would declare proudly, "Rose." The names changed: Catherine, Maria, Deborah. Sometimes Puente said the children were her adopted daughters, although she never went through any legal process to make it so. In her own mind, the dozen or more little girls were her children, stand-ins for the two real daughters she had given away and lost track of entirely.

Puente wanted her lawyer to take care of all kinds of legal problems for the girls and their parents. Credit problems, divorces, bankruptcies, she paid for all of them. The impression Dorothea Puente made on these people, especially the girls, was deep and loving. Later, as grown women, many credited Puente with saving them from jail or death.

She showed them how a caring, motherly person acted and spoke. She instilled self-reliance, a strong sense of femininity. "You are in my mind and my heart," one now grown-up protégée of Puente's from those years said recently. Another summed up the feelings of all of them: "I just hate to think about where I would be today if this woman had not touched my life."

Puente, always hard to unravel, was a contradictory collection of compassionate impulses and radical selfishness. These were contradictions that grew worse, more extreme, as the years went on.

Around 1977, Puente entered a hospital for surgery. Her weight had grown morbid and she needed a jejunal-ileo bypass to close part of her intestine to prevent her from gaining more weight and to shed a lot as well. As she had done since childhood, Puente exaggerated the illness. She had told visitors to 2100 F Street that she had a fatal heart disease and various forms of cancer. The only real cancer she had was a basal cell growth on the tip of her nose, which was treated successfully. She did have her thyroid removed, leaving a neck scar, but her health was actually quite good, given the amount of alcohol and stress she subjected herself to.

Puente summoned her lawyer to her hospital bedside before her corrective surgery. She had asked the Seventh-Day Adventists, who sent tenants to her, to pray for her. She told them she was going to die.

Propped up in bed, alternately feeble, then domineering, Puente ordered her lawyer to draw up a will. She named each of her "stepdaughters" with a bequest. Then she set up educational scholarships for them. Her lawyer dutifully scratched down the will. It was a document fit for a grand lady, a political force, a wealthy woman who had homes everywhere.

The catch lay in the fact that Puente had nowhere near the money needed to actually make the bequests. It was another fantasy. She did have money, but it was all stolen. At $200 to $300 per month per tenant, Puente had been keeping most of the assistance checks sent to her tenants, using the cash to finance her grand style in politics and her charities. Her alcoholic tenants got only room and board while she took their money.

After her operation she went back to 2100 F Street. By now her dreams of glamour and the financial demands on her were getting out of hand. A day of accounting was drawing down on her.

But before the blow fell, Dorothea Puente fell in love and married for the fourth and last time.

Puente had started noticing a young Mexican laborer working the grounds at 2100 F Street. His name was Pedro Angel Montalvo. He was bouncy, almost too high-strung and excitable, and by July 1975 he had lived at the boardinghouse for a year. Puente began spending more time with him, inviting him to the third floor, taking him to her favorite bars. She even introduced him to some of the management of the business, careful to keep all of the financial pieces in her own hands.

They got married in 1976, again for Puente, in Reno. Montalvo apparently started having second thoughts as soon as the ceremony was over. Dorothea was about ten years his senior, yet she wavered strangely between acting much older, especially for visiting social workers, or trying to act much younger. She had a constant need for clothes, trips to the beauty parlor, shoes.

As for Montalvo, he did not impress others. Puente's lawyer Dorfman candidly thought Montalvo was crazy, jumping around the office, talking loudly, bragging, acting excitable. The physician who saw the tenants at 2100 F Street agreed with Dorfman. He believed Montalvo had married this chunky, tale-spinning older woman simply to get permanent residence in the United States and access to her money and her car. Both men, like others who observed Dorothea Puente at this time, were utterly amazed that the sober, if quaintly fibbing woman, who mothered and bossed others, would marry someone so different from herself.

Montalvo had his own worries. He believed that his new wife was lying about her wealth. She lived as if she were rich, but he suspected she was stealing to support her grandeur.

As she had with Roberto Puente, Dorothea started quarreling with Montalvo at once. They separated soon after the Reno ceremony, got together again briefly, and then Montalvo agreed to an annulment. If he hoped to tap into a rich woman, he had struck fool's gold instead.

Dorothea Puente claimed Montalvo was physically abusive from the moment they were married. He beat her, she said, and stabbed her between the eyes. In their first married week, she alleged that Montalvo killed her pet cat, broke windows at 2100 F Street, and slashed the tires of her car. However much of this was invention, theirs was not a happy marriage, and Dorothea Puente was certainly incapable of having one. Her pattern, from McFaul through Montalvo was invariant, and always replayed the scenes she had been part of between her own father and Trudy. So in 1982 when she wrote to a judge, seeking leniency, she wrote with absolute falsity, "All my problems started when I married Mr. Montalvo." They were much older, more intractable than a sour late-life marriage could cause.

Through the harrowing stress of running a business, playing mother to surrogate daughters, sponsoring Hispanic causes, Puente also whisked in and out of homes as a nurse. She stole small things, sometimes checks, from her sick or elderly patients. But she always came through the door with a smile.

Everyone—bartenders, cabdrivers, tenants, social workers, and her housebound patients—praised her. A portrait of Puente, describing her at this point in her life, appeared later in a Sacramento magazine: "She was an attractive woman, striking some would say. She had the countenance of a fairy godmother and Florence Nightingale rolled into one. Her silvery hair was perfectly in place, her stylish clothes fit well . . . [she] always had a pleasant word for everybody even though she herself, poor thing, was suffering from cancer." The last comment was, of course, a sarcastic reference to Puente's susceptibility to sympathy-attracting diseases.

This strange, wonderful figure lived in a dreamy state herself. One of her "stepdaughters" loved going into Puente's bedroom. It was the prettiest room in the house at 2100 F Street, ladylike, frilly, soft, with drapes and curtains and bright pillows. It made the young girl feel like Cinderella, an effect Puente enjoyed too.

But in mid-September 1978, Dorothea Puente's dream life and real life came tumbling down. The Social Security Administration had started an investigation of forged checks paid to her and turned the matter over to the Treasury Department. Until then no one in authority had bothered to ask how a woman who'd been convicted of forgery and prostitution could reliably run a boardinghouse for alcoholics on government assistance.

Now the questions were being sharply asked, and the answers set in motion a murderous series of events that ended on a rainy Friday morning in the muddy ground at 1426 F Street ten years later.

11

THE IRONY WAS THAT PUENTE WAS BROUGHT DOWN BY A JAIL inmate, someone as familiar with a cell as she was.

Robert Davis was doing time at the county's Rio Consumnes Correctional Center in 1977. He had been living at 2100 F Street for about three years, and he'd spent time in and out of county jail for minor offenses. He was in jail, waiting for his Social Security check and got very angry when it was late, and angrier still when it turned up with his signature on it. He had never seen it until after it was cashed.

The ensuing Treasury Department investigation uncovered thirty-four more checks to tenants at 2100 F Street, all with forged signatures. And all of the signatures were written by one hand: Dorothea Puente, the socialite and political gadfly.

When questioned by Treasury agents, Puente said that Robert Davis had asked her to come out to RCCC and bring his check. "He asked me to cash it for him. I went there to have him sign it." Puente puffed up defiantly. "The guards were standing right there while Davis signed the check over to me."

It was an audacious lie, but typical of Puente.

So Pedro Montalvo, whom all of Puente's professional associates considered a kook, had been right after all. She was an outright thief.

The Treasury Department did not probe every transaction Puente had conducted over her years at 2100 F Street and stopped totaling forgeries when they got to about $4,000. It was enough for a felony conviction.

As she had in the past, Puente hated going to trial, and so pled guilty to federal forgery. Because of her age and the nonviolent nature of the crime, she was not sent to prison. Instead, she was put on five years formal parole and ordered to undergo psychiatric counseling.

The last condition of parole was a wise one. Puente suffered what amounted to a nervous breakdown in 1978 because of her conviction.

Crying constantly, confused, angry, dazed, Puente kept up her appointments with her parole agent and always dressed very well, but she had trouble living from day to day. As part of the plea bargain, she was forced to give up 2100 F Street, lost her position as a civic leader, and was now shunned by the political figures who had courted her and kissed her so publicly.

Suddenly she was nothing and nobody. And worse, she had no money and no grand house or staff. Her life may have been mostly lies, bought with stolen money, but some of it was real. Now it was all gone, the truth and lies alike.

She took odd jobs again, as if starting over. Dishwashing, cleaning, cooking—menial jobs for people she thought below her. She could do nothing for her "stepdaughters" or the Hispanic artists she cultivated.

Puente left Sacramento, going south to Stockton. She lived alone, going to bars at night, still elegant outwardly, but struggling mightily to maintain the mask. She was brooding a lot. She had been stupid to make herself so vulnerable, to put herself in a position where everything could be taken away from her.

Next time it would be different. She blamed the whole thing on Montalvo, as she told a judge in 1982. "It was during this time I started writing checks," she said brazenly, ignoring years of previous criminality and forgery. "I just wanted you to know I'm not a street bum."

She also began seeing a psychiatrist for the first time. He was appointed by the federal court and it was a fateful pairing for Puente and him. Dr. Thomas Doody became enmeshed in her life from 1978 until 1989 when he found himself, because of her, in court, trying to maintain the confidentiality of his patients.

But what Dr. Doody first observed in 1978 was a seriously unbalanced personality. She was, he wrote, "a schizophrenic, chronic undifferentiated type." It was a catch-all diagnosis, merely saying that Puente had a severe emotional problem. The truth was, over the years, that Dr. Doody really had no clear idea what he had on his hands. Dorothea Puente was unlike any patient he had seen in nearly twenty years of practice. No one matched her ability to lie, manipulate, and deceive.

Even while she was cooperating with the court, seeing her parole agent and a psychiatrist, Puente could not resist forgery. In 1978 in Stockton she passed another Treasury check. She made repayment quickly and there was no prosecution. The incident should have signaled that even in the most dire circumstances, Dorothea Puente would break the law if she thought it would help her. But she was being so helpful that her latest criminal act was overlooked.

She disliked Stockton, a smaller, cramped city compared to Sacramento, and in mid-1979 she went north again. She had apparently decided to concentrate on individuals rather than a big operation like 2100 F Street. She would be a nurse.

And she had also apparently decided that she would risk

much more than a few months in jail rather than lose her money, dreams, and respect again.

Ricardo Odorica was a small man, not quite five feet tall, with black hair, and a wizened, prematurely aged face. He had come from Mexico in 1967, met his future wife, Veronica, and had married. They both had been born in Zacatecas.

Odorica got one of his first jobs in California at the Mansion Inn, which later became the Clarion Hotel. He worked long hours as a gardener. He and Veronica saved their money, did without trips or luxuries. By 1975, Odorica had saved enough to buy the family's first home, a run-down two-story Victorian at 1426 F Street.

He and Veronica worked on the house for years, fixing the buckled floors, the cracked walls, planting flowers, painting. They spent their time on the first floor, living there with their two young daughters. The second floor remained a mess.

At night, after work, Odorica sometimes went over to Joe's Corner for a drink. Veronica often didn't join him. He was sitting there one night in 1979, drinking a beer, when a silver-haired, kindly woman approached him. She was dressed beautifully. "I heard that the second floor of your house is for rent," she said.

Odorica was dazzled by the genteel, well-bred woman. She was charming, smart, and she liked him. "The second floor's in terrible shape," he stammered to her.

"I'd like to rent it."

"Are you sure? You haven't even seen it."

"I like the neighborhood. I used to live near here," she told him.

They walked the two doors from the bar to 1426 F Street. The woman, whom Odorica called "the lady" as if she were royalty, said her name was Dorothea Montalvo. She made an immediate impression on Veronica and the two little girls. She chatted sweetly with them, hugged them, talked intelligently about her medical training. She promised to help Veronica with tips about getting the best schooling and clothes for the kids.

Odorica thought a fairy godmother had walked into his life.

She rented the second floor for $200 a month and moved right in. Dorothea began making small improvements on the second floor, adding a decent bed and bureaus, trying to turn the peeling, dusty apartment into a version of her rooms at 2100 F Street.

She spent many nights with Veronica when Ricardo was at work, babysitting the little girls, tutoring them in English, gently chatting with them in Spanish. Dorothea said that she had been very wealthy and that Pedro Montalvo had stolen all of her money. "I've lived in castles," she told Veronica and Ricardo soon after they met, "but I'll sleep on the floor if I have to." She told them about her fine house in Cuernavaca, and the many relatives in Mexico, of her ex-husbands, all of whom she said she supported.

Ricardo and Veronica were so entranced by the grandmotherly and warm older woman that they asked her to be the sponsor for one of their daughters at her first Holy Communion. Dorothea was with the Odoricas for almost every holiday meal, for almost every dinner, and for every special occasion like a christening. She became, in very short order, one of the family.

For Dorothea Puente, the Odoricas represented a vision of family life she never had, and a ready conduit for money that she herself, as a parolee and ex-con, would have had trouble explaining to authorities. She was also not above using her new friend Ricardo as an accomplice.

Where had penniless, but ruthless Dorothea Puente gotten money not only to rent from the Odoricas but to buy things for herself?

Since her return to Sacramento, besides doing odd jobs as a cook or dishwasher, she had occupied her time going from one private nursing business to another, passing herself off as a trained live-in caretaker for the sick or elderly. She had the brusque professionalism, the matronly stance, of a longtime nurse. Several businesses bonded her, meaning they vouched for her bona fides. They did not, though, do any background checks on Puente. No one knew she was an ex-con on parole.

So she was sent out to feed and clean up after vulnerable, older shut-ins. Rumors began that she was stealing from some of them, little things that would not be missed or chalked up to fading, elderly memories.

But in one house, Dorothea Puente found someone she could control and steal from. And Puente was willing to cross over the line to harming people.

For the first time, social workers who had been so fond of Puente started believing she was capable of murder.

12

SOMETHING TERRIBLE WAS WRONG WITH ESTHER BUSBY. HER doctor thought so; her social worker, Mildred Ballenger, did, too. But no one could figure out what was happening. Busby's kindly nurse Dorothea seemed always distraught and worried when the old woman became suddenly sick.

Busby was in her seventies, a frail, smallish woman with a generally bright temperament, living in a small home. She was cared for by Dr. Jerome Lackner, who had been Director for Public Health in California under Governor Jerry Brown. With a handlebar mustache, abrupt manners, Lackner was an alert, careful doctor who knew his patient was in the grip of something very odd.

In late 1979, Dorothea Montalvo had started providing live-in nursing for Busby. The job required Dorothea to sleep in Mrs. Busby's house. By early 1980, things started happening.

Busby was frequently admitted to Sutter General Hospital for emergency treatment of medical problems that had no suspicious cause. Dr. Lackner certainly never noted one.

Mildred Ballenger was curious. She began keeping track of Busby's acute attacks. Large, open, with gray hair, Ballenger was Lackner's equivalent, keenly aware of her clients' well-being and tenacious on their behalf. Once Busby got to the hospital, Lackner and other doctors would stabilize her and her condition would improve almost overnight; the source of the medical problem stayed unknown. Busby herself was frightened and bewildered. She was old but not stupid. She tried frantically to get someone—her doctor, her social worker—to tell her what was going on. No one knew.

One telling fact emerged. Busby, getting better in her hospital room, would relapse into medical emergencies soon after solicitous visits of Dorothea Montalvo. The doctors would rush in, get Busby's heart beating normally, her breathing regular, and the crisis would pass. She rebounded quickly, too, and was discharged and sent home.

But, soon after she got home, with Dorothea feeding and medicating her daily, Mrs. Busby suddenly fell ill and would have to be brought, by speeding ambulance, back to Sutter General.

Mildred Ballenger worked for Adult Protective Services and felt her professional duty required her to dig deeper into the peculiar pattern of Esther Busby's hospitalizations. She called Peggy Rossi, who was responsible at Sutter General for scrutinizing the discharge records of elderly, potentially vulnerable people like Mrs. Busby.

"What's going on?" Ballenger asked pointedly.

Rossi checked her records. "I don't know. Everything should be fine. Mrs. Busby's getting her medication regularly, she's fed. With a caretaker like Dorothea, I don't understand it."

Ballenger chose her words carefully. "I've been hearing rumors from my other clients. About Dorothea. She uses different names. That may not even be her name."

"What rumors?"

"She poisoned her last two husbands."

"Oh, my God."

"It hasn't been proven," Ballenger said. "But don't Esther's illnesses sound like poisoning?"

Rossi said, "I'll call Dr. Lackner."

Lackner, after talking to Rossi, was perplexed. Busby's emergencies had all been attributable to some prosaic cause: too much salt in her food, too much digitalis, her heart medicine. An overdose of salt, for a woman with Busby's fragile heart, could be fatal. Too much digitalis, instead of stimulating her heart, could stop it. If this was poisoning, it was diabolically clever and simple. The victim had access to these substances herself.

But what about this Dorothea Montalvo? Lackner recalled how Dorothea always came with Mrs. Busby when she was rushed into the emergency room, then followed along to her hospital bedside. How is she, will she get better? The poor woman, how terrible, Dorothea wrung her hands, begged to help. What can I do, tell me, Dorothea would plead, her face contorted with worry.

Dorothea was in and out of Mrs. Busby's room all the time. She was, Lackner thought, the perfect friend to Busby. *I wish every elderly patient had a friend like this, someone to look out for them,* Lackner thought as he watched Dorothea bustling into the room.

He was familiar with Montalvo, too. She had been his patient for a short time and he treated her for potassium retention, an ulcerlike condition, and heartbeat irregularities. She did not take digitalis, though.

But Lackner changed his mind. Busby kept going into the hospital and he kept thinking about Rossi and Ballenger's fears. It was, he realized, only by the grace of God that Esther Busby didn't die in the emergency room. The next "illness" could kill her.

Plaintively, Mrs. Busby asked her doctor, "What's wrong with me?" and he couldn't answer her.

Lackner startlingly concluded that Dorothea wasn't worried about Busby's health during those tearful, hand-wringing visits at the hospital. She was worried Busby would recover completely. She's got Esther at home or in the hospital, he thought, keeping her alive, but sick so she's got access to everything, checks, whoever came by. It was an ideal setup for cold blooded theft.

Lackner paid a visit to Mrs. Busby after her recovery from one of the strange medical episodes. Esther was apparently not suspicious of Dorothea and liked having her there at home.

Dorothea proudly said to Lackner, "I make sure she takes her digitalis on schedule," pointing to the table of medicines for Esther Busby.

Later, Lackner presumed that Dorothea didn't show him everything she was dosing Busby with.

His home visit had aroused Dorothea Puente's keen sense of danger. The next time Mrs. Busby had an emergency illness, Lackner was surprised to find his patient rushed to the University of California at Davis Medical Center about twenty miles away rather than to the much closer Sutter General. Lackner realized why immediately. At UCDMC Busby was a new patient and the treating physicians wouldn't be suspicious of her unusual illnesses. Dorothea could start her lies all over with a fresh audience.

He talked again to Peggy Rossi, reporting the odd development.

Rossi said, "Esther Busby's being poisoned."

Like a bolt, Lackner saw it all. "My God, Peg, that's exactly what's going on."

At UCDMC, the doctors and nurses had quickly observed a marked deterioration in Busby's condition following visits by Dorothea Puente.

Lackner got a call from a friend at the hospital to discuss his sick patient. "I want you to run a tox screen to see what's in her blood," Lackner said. He believed a toxicological examination would show something.

Sure enough, Busby's blood contained phenobarbitol, a drug he had never prescribed for her. This fitted Busby's comalike appearance whenever she first arrived at the hospital, too. Lackner was certain Busby was being poisoned when the tox screen showed digoxin in her blood. Digoxin was a heart medication, not prescribed for Esther Busby but being taken by Dorothea Puente.

Lackner and Ballenger heard that Puente was calling Mrs. Busby's relatives, telling them the old woman had terminal cancer and more money was immediately needed for her care. She doesn't have cancer, Lackner thought. Dorothea's lying. *To get the money.*

When he knew Dorothea would be out, Lackner went to see Mrs. Busby. Bluntly he told her that she had high levels of a strange medication in her system. He said Dorothea was poisoning her. "She's calling your family, too. She says you're dying and need money," Lackner told Mrs. Busby.

Frightened and angry, the old woman asked, "What should I do?"

"Fire her," Lackner answered.

Mrs. Busby nodded. Dorothea Puente was dismissed immediately to her shocked, quarrelsome chagrin.

There is no indication that anyone contacted the private nursing companies that continued to send Dorothea out to see patients. Puente's homicidal career is a record not so much of her unmasking, as her slipping away from pursuers.

She had taken on two dedicated foes in 1980, Lackner and especially Ballenger. Working on parallel tracks, they notified the Sacramento Police Department that a dangerous woman was loose among sick people.

The tip came to Sergeant Dave Schwartz in Homicide. Slight, self-confident, with a thin black mustache, Schwartz heard all of the suspicions Lackner and Ballenger had documented and built up. He agreed that Dorothea Puente's behavior looked sinister and that she might have been poisoning Esther Busby, but these suspicions wouldn't support sending the matter to the DA's office or doing much more. It was mostly conjecture.

When Esther Busby died in a nursing home in 1981, Schwartz reported her death as possibly suspicious, and noted that the woman's doctor and others thought she had been poisoned in the past. Schwartz, like Lackner and Ballenger, intended to keep an eye on the busy, courteous, and grandmotherly Dorothea Puente.

In 1980 Dr. Thomas Coyle at Sutter General began noticing that one of his patients had an unusual pattern of acute illnesses and recovery. He made a note in his medical record that it looked like intentional poisoning.

The patient, an elderly, generally solitary woman like Busby, didn't get better. Coyle talked to Peggy Rossi about the case. Very quickly Rossi's fears were heightened. "Is someone looking after this woman?" she asked.

"She's got an attendant. She got her through an agency, a bonded one. I don't remember the woman's name offhand."

Rossi thought, don't tell me it's Montalvo.

She told the doctor it was imperative to find out who was looking after this elderly woman. Coyle and Rossi hurried to the patient's room. "I think the attendant's name is in this address book," the doctor said, picking up a slim book on the bedside table.

Rossi fearfully waited as they checked. Under *M,* they found the name Dorothea Montalvo, 1426 F Street.

Rossi hurried back to her office and called the Nursing Office at the hospital. She was angry that another elderly woman had fallen into Dorothea's web. "I want Montalvo reported for poisoning this woman," Rossi said emphatically.

But the Nursing Office, unpersuaded, refused, based on the scanty information, to take any steps against Dorothea.

Shaking her head, angry, frustrated, Rossi placed an anonymous call to Mildred Ballenger, who had made no secret of her accusations about Dorothea Puente. Rossi told Ballenger that another old woman was being poisoned.

Ballenger wasted no time. The patient was told, just as Busby had been, and Puente was fired.

Ballenger made it a point to keep Schwartz at SPD apprised of what Puente was doing, where she went, what patients she saw. Maybe they could catch her in the act, or at least prevent something fatal from happening.

A bitter Ballenger found her path blocked at the county counsel's office when she reported Puente. The county counsel refused to go to the Sacramento County Welfare Department to have Puente barred from working with the sick and dependent. The answer was the same one Rossi had gotten: not enough information.

What Ballenger did accomplish over the next year, was to turn up four more patients of Puente's who experienced health emergencies under her care. One woman, according to Ballenger, died after repeated heart attacks "within minutes" of eating or drinking food Dorothea had prepared for her. Still, Schwartz wearily insisted that the link from Puente to poisoning was too tenuous to justify arresting her.

Mildred Ballenger, tracking Puente like a Fury, and Schwartz realized that what they needed was for Puente to be caught pouring something into someone's food or actually seen stealing from someone's home or passing a forged check.

In early 1982, Ballenger and Schwartz got all three from an unwittingly obliging Dorothea Puente.

PART 3

Night air and gardening are the great tonics. There is nothing so stimulating as bare contact with rich mother earth. You are never so fresh as when you have been grubbing in the soil—black hands, black nails, and boots covered with mud.

E. F. Benson,
"Mrs. Amworth"

13

"KEEP AN EYE ON HER," DAVE SCHWARTZ WARNED ME ON MARCH 2, 1982. "She's dangerous. I haven't even sent over the good case yet."

He meant Dorothea Montalvo and the series of cases he was then submitting to the Sacramento County District Attorney for prosecution. Puente, then using the Montalvo name, had been very busy in early 1982 and through the spring and her tenacious enemies, Ballenger and Schwartz, had finally caught up with her.

The Homicide detective wanted to avoid letting a deputy DA like me get fooled by Montalvo as so many had been before. I sat in my office, poring over the files that started showing up on her, chilled by the almost vampiric parasitism of this seemingly gentle white-haired grandmother. She really was like Benson's vampire, Mrs. Amworth, who looked like a jolly, motherly woman and trapped her victims through deception.

In 1982 I had been with the DA's office for about five years, handling everything from disturbing the peace to murder. I had quit in 1981 to write full-time. Then about a year later, the office needed an immediate replacement for about eight months for a deputy going on maternity leave. Although I wanted to write as a career, I was still close enough to the good spirits, high-mindedness, competitive routine, and courtroom antics to want to continue as a DA for a little longer.

So I ended up with Dorothea Montalvo Puente by accident.

The office felony bureau was divided into five trial teams. I was assigned to Team Four. Tim Frawley, my old law school friend, was the supervisor and he sent me the more volatile cases, the ones which might require special handling, like Montalvo. I could devote the time to them unlike a regular deputy. Since I was only going to be in the office a short time, Frawley knew my judgment would be unclouded by thoughts of career advancement.

Team Four was a cluttered crush of little offices on the third floor of the squat, very ugly new building the DA had moved into from the courthouse across the street. The courthouse was an enormous white rectangle without exterior decoration, like the most graceless, cold hospital imaginable. The Montalvo crimes would play themselves out in courtrooms in that coldness.

"Don't drop the ball on this one," Schwartz admonished me over the phone in March. "There's a lot more going on than you think. She's worth the time."

I discovered, through the files, that Dorothea Montalvo had been very active lately. She moved like a shark among the older, weaker people in downtown Sacramento.

The first case I saw established Montalvo's capacity for predatory heartlessness.

Malcolm McKenzie went out drinking at the Zebra Club in late January. In his seventies, McKenzie enjoyed going to bars, and he was a regular at the Zebra Club. He was a two-drink customer, lingering and talking for hours.

On the night he sat down near the door, McKenzie was

delighted when an attractive, very well dressed older woman came in and struck up a conversation. She swept into the bar, her manners and brightness almost out of place among the usual drinkers. She told McKenzie her name was Dorothea. They moved to the bar. It was late in the evening and they had time only for two drinks. McKenzie let Dorothea know that his apartment was nearby.

"I'd like to see it," she said, flattering him with attention.

"Well, let's go," McKenzie said happily. The bartender saw them get into a cab.

By the time they got to his apartment, McKenzie felt distinctly unwell, strange. He had never experienced sensations like this before, a paralytic numbness that froze his arms and legs. As Dorothea stood over him, he lay down on the sofa. In another moment, McKenzie found he couldn't move his body at all. He was conscious, able to see and hear, but he couldn't talk.

He watched in stunned amazement as Dorothea began a thorough, businesslike search of his apartment. She opened drawers, went through closets, checked his clothes. She found a small red suitcase and started putting things into it, including a collection of wheat pennies worth some money. Smaller items, like cash, she just stuffed into her pockets.

Then McKenzie saw her glance around and come toward him. She grabbed his left hand and tugged at his pinky ring, finally pulling it free. McKenzie couldn't resist in any way. With a last, acquisitive look around the apartment, Dorothea, red suitcase in hand, left as casually as if nothing had happened.

McKenzie stayed frozen on the sofa for another hour, then found he could move a little, got to the telephone, and called the police.

It hadn't taken long for the police to catch up with Montalvo after that. She tried to pass two of McKenzie's checks at Joe's Corner several days later. "He gave them to me," she insisted to the police, even though only her handwriting appeared on the checks. She claimed to be seventy-two years old. She was really only fifty-three, but her appearance matched that of a much older woman. "This man wanted to go steady with me," Montalvo said, "but I wouldn't do it. I didn't take anything from him."

But she hedged. "I've got a psychiatric condition. I sometimes forget my actions." She said she was being treated.

I went to Frawley's office on the second floor. "What's so special about this?"

Frawley leaned back. "It didn't look like much to me. Dave Schwartz called me. He says she's very dangerous and he's got a lot more cases coming over."

Frawley said that Schwartz was also talking to George Williamson, who was in Special Investigations in the DA's office. "We'll have to handle her carefully," Frawley told me.

I wondered why Schwartz, a Homicide detective, was so interested in a thief. I got a better idea when her other crimes popped up.

Not long after apparently drugging and robbing Malcolm McKenzie, Montalvo struck at an eighty-two-year-old woman living alone at the St. Francis Mansion.

Irene Gregory was frail, ill, and needed outside help to get through the day's routine. One morning in the spring of 1982 she was visited by a kindly, professional-sounding woman named Betty Peterson. "I'm from the Sacramento Medical Association," the white-haired woman, wearing glasses, carrying a medical bag, told Mrs. Gregory. But Betty Peterson also looked odd. She wore a floral-print dress and a lot of makeup, her nails painted a flashy, loud red. She said she was a nurse and she had come to help Mrs. Gregory. She even produced medical gear and competently took Mrs. Gregory's blood pressure. Betty Peterson looked, sounded, and acted like a genuine nurse, perhaps a slightly eccentric one.

Mrs. Gregory had seen this nurse before. One of the few things Irene Gregory did regularly was go to Marcene's Beauty Parlor to get her hair done. On a recent trip, Mrs. Gregory had fallen down as she got out of the chair, and

Betty Peterson had been there to help her up, check her for bruises, comfort her, and get her address in case there were further problems. Mrs. Gregory had a granddaughter and a small circle of friends who looked out for her, but she was by herself a lot of the time.

"How are you feeling after that fall?" the nurse asked, putting away the blood pressure gauge.

"Oh, better. It wasn't really too bad."

Peterson was sympathetic and nodded. She said, "Well, I think I have something for you," Peterson said. "Your blood pressure tells me that you're keeping too much water. You need to get rid of it to feel better and recover faster."

Mrs. Gregory nodded. Peterson pulled out a bottle of pills from her medical bag. "I know your doctor," and she named Mrs. Gregory's treating physician. It wasn't unusual for her to know the name: the doctor's medications were nearby on tables in the apartment.

"These are water pills," Peterson told Mrs. Gregory. "Take a couple of them and lie down."

Dutifully, Mrs. Gregory swallowed the pills. She watched the smiling, reassuring nurse. Then Mrs. Gregory lost consciousness.

When she woke up, hours had passed. Betty Peterson was gone along with a valuable diamond ring in an elaborate setting and about one hundred Dalmane pills Mrs. Gregory took as medication.

Feeling faint, Mrs. Gregory stumbled to the telephone and called her granddaughter. Then the two of them reported the incident to the police. The problem was that Mrs. Gregory couldn't identify Betty Peterson beyond giving a description.

But luck was with Irene Gregory. Several days later she went back to Marcene's to have her hair shampooed and set. Sitting in a chair, bold and brazen, was the false nurse, Peterson. "Call the police," Mrs. Gregory spluttered, but before SPD arrived, a perfectly calm Betty Peterson got up, tidied herself, and walked out after telling her hairdresser that she was going to Mexico.

The hairdresser, though, knew Peterson's real name was Dorothea Montalvo, and the police quickly arrested her at 1426 F Street. Montalvo maintained she had done nothing, and none of Irene Gregory's jewelry was ever found. The whole experience shook Mrs. Gregory to her core. She locked her door tightly at the St. Francis Mansion, was fearful of going out, and terrified of people.

This Montalvo, I realized, was a very special criminal. It took a rare callousness to drug two old people and steal the rings off their fingers.

Then Schwartz called and solved the puzzle of his interest in Montalvo. "We're pretty sure she killed someone," he said. "The problem is we probably can't ever prove it."

"The case is bad?" I asked, ready to credit almost anything to Dorothea Montalvo.

"There's a lot of possibilities, but there's nothing to work up. I just wanted you to know about it."

"Who was it?"

"A sick lady, someone she was working for," Schwartz said sourly. "Like the ones you're getting now."

I didn't know it for several months, but he was talking about Esther Busby. "Are there more cases coming?"

"You bet. We're digging back, too. I bet we find some old ones she's good for."

In rapid succession, more Dorothea Montalvo crimes appeared.

Claire Maleville and Lauretta Chalmers were elderly women who employed Montalvo as a live-in attendant or occasional helper. The two old women never met each other, but their identical experiences bound them together. Montalvo was working through the Quality Care Nursing Agency, apparently a reputable, trustworthy person to have around old people. But both Maleville and Chalmers discovered checks and personal belongings missing after Montalvo was in their homes. The checks began appearing with forged signatures on them.

I was starting to set up court dates to put Montalvo's

crimes in front of a judge. In California the first step in taking a serious crime, a felony, to trial, is a preliminary hearing held in a lower court, the municipal court, before a judge without a jury. My job was to present just enough evidence at the hearing to show that a crime had been committed and that the defendant likely committed it. The case would then be sent to superior court for trial.

But Maleville and Chalmers showed me how hard it was going to be to nail Dorothea Montalvo.

Claire Maleville called me first, days before the preliminary hearing. "I'm so sorry," she said, her voice thin and quavery. "I simply can't come to court."

"You're the only one who can tell the judge that Montalvo took your checks without permission."

"And if I don't testify?"

"Well, the judge needs to hear from the victim, Mrs. Maleville. Without you, I have to dismiss this charge." I hated pressuring the infirm, nervous, and fearful old woman.

"Can't I just send in a statement? She did steal those checks from me."

I explained the law of forgery. "You have to be on the witness stand, so you can be cross-examined, too."

"I can't do that," Mrs. Maleville said anxiously. "I'm far too ill. I'm in bed all the time."

She apologized again and again. I had her under subpoena but I couldn't force a sick old woman into court. Lauretta Chalmers called soon afterward. She, too, was bedridden and unable to make it to court. Suddenly the Montalvo prosecution was coming apart.

The police had uncovered an earlier crime, committed in August 1981. It was the same story. Dorothy Gosling, eighty-four years old, hired Montalvo as a nurse and cook. Then the elderly woman discovered $3,500 worth of gold rings and other jewelry missing. Montalvo had the run of the house, preparing meals, cleaning up, conscientiously tending to Mrs. Gosling. But several times, Mrs. Gosling went to bed and woke up later to find more of her possessions gone, including checks. The pattern of deep, sudden sleep followed by missing property looked suspect, too. Schwartz said that no drugs were found in Mrs. Gosling's system, though. In 1981 the police hadn't been looking that closely for drugs.

I didn't have any drugs at all to show a judge, much less a jury later. I only had people who ate or drank near Montalvo, lost consciousness or their ability to move, and later found they'd been robbed.

When Mrs. Gosling pleaded with me in early April that she too couldn't stand the strain of coming to court, I was left with Malcolm McKenzie. The preliminary hearing was scheduled for April 12. The appalling possibility existed that Montalvo, having chosen her weak, helpless victims so well, would benefit from their frailty and walk away free.

14

If I was feeling pressure as the preliminary hearing got nearer, so was Dorothea Montalvo.

Since January 1982 she had been arrested four times, and now faced a long prison sentence if convicted. Each time she was arrested her bail rose, from $15,000 to $30,000. She had to keep finding more money on very short notice if she wanted to stay out of custody until the preliminary hearing.

I tried to make her life as miserable as possible that spring.

My own life wasn't happy. After talking with George Williamson, who was also tracking the Montalvo cases in the DA's office, we concluded that there was no way to get legally useful testimony from the reluctant, sick old victims. My only hope was to use McKenzie to send Montalvo to trial, buy some time to re-file or shore up the other cases. As Schwartz and Mildred Ballenger reminded me several times, Montalvo had to be taken off the streets.

It was with a lot of relief that I brought Malcolm McKenzie into my office the morning of April 12.

He turned out to be a spry, bright-eyed man in white pants and a white windbreaker. His gray hair was carefully combed and he smiled often. He seemed high-spirited.

We went over the limited purpose of the hearing. I told McKenzie I wouldn't ask him every possible question. He got a little nervous thinking about cross-examination, but perked up quickly.

"Is she going to be there?" he asked.

"If she is, I'm going to have her arrested after the prelim," I said.

He grinned. "That should be fun. Is it on my charges?"

"No. We turned up some more checks she'd written." I didn't tell McKenzie that he was the single thread keeping the Montalvo prosecution together. I gathered up my files, took McKenzie in hand, and we walked across the street to the courthouse. I hoped for the best.

The schedule of cases in a criminal court is called the calendar. Morning calendars in Department D were crowded, noisy, chaotic. I left McKenzie in the courtroom's audience section. He stood out in his white outfit among the children, darker clothes, the mass of sour-faced people waiting for court to start.

I needed to find Montalvo's lawyer. The time had come to try for a deal, since I only had one victim available.

Al Hess, Montalvo's public defender, had been a criminal lawyer for years. He wore glasses, slouched a little, and had a cynical smile. "Are we going to get rid of this?" Hess asked me. He never looked like he took his cases seriously, but he was an effective trial lawyer.

"Is she here?" I asked. I thought she might avoid court.

"Didn't you see her coming in?" Al grinned wryly. "She's the little old lady, the sweet one sitting in front."

"She can plead to a four-eight-seven point two straight up," I said, bluffing a little. I was offering a guilty plea to grand theft from the person of McKenzie, short of robbery with force. It was a felony and Montalvo probably would go to prison.

Hess knew a bluff. He snorted dismissively. "She won't take it. You have your victim?"

I nodded. Hess wanted to see McKenzie testify before accepting any plea bargain. Maybe he could walk Montalvo free completely. He already knew, because I had told him, that I couldn't produce the other victims that morning.

"He gave her the stuff," Hess said. "He just doesn't remember. They got drunk together. Look, the judge's going to drop this down to a misdemeanor after the prelim."

"No deal for a misdemeanor," I said.

Hess shrugged. Montalvo was merely another case in the pile of files he carried that morning. "Let's see the judge."

As we walked into the judge's chambers, I passed Montalvo for the first time. She wore a black dress, her white hair in a grandmotherly bun. She was stout, pale-skinned, with glasses, as meek and harmless-looking as Mrs. Butterworth on the maple syrup bottles.

There was a mob of lawyers, all talking, in the judge's chambers. The judge was Kate Canlis, a bright, sharp-tongued former deputy DA I had known for a long time. She was trying to work out which prelims would actually go to a hearing and which would plead.

She gave me a fish-eye. "Why are you going after that cute little old lady?" she demanded.

"Wait until you hear my witness."

Canlis turned to Hess. "Is she going to take anything?"

Hess shook his head. "I asked her. She says she hasn't done anything. No deal." He smiled at the judge. "You'll drop it down to a misdemeanor after you hear the prelim anyway."

"Maybe, Mr. Hess," Canlis said, moving to another case and another brace of bickering lawyers in front of her.

Back in court I was annoyed and nervous. Canlis might decide that Montalvo had done very little or that McKenzie was confused, or McKenzie might freeze on the witness stand. Anything could happen. I would have to dismiss the last case, arrest Montalvo outside of the courtroom on additional forged checks, and then re-file everything and try for a second and last time. In California, the prosecution could re-file a case only once after dismissal.

That would leave Dorothea Montalvo on the street, free to roam among the gullible and vulnerable.

There was almost no one left in Canlis's courtroom when *People v. Dorothea Montalvo* was called. Still fussing with a small purse, as she had while waiting for the case, Montalvo sat down beside Hess at the counsel table. Canlis, sitting on the bench, told me to call my first witness.

I asked for Malcolm McKenzie. He came forward, a little jittery, took the oath, and sat down on the witness stand. Montalvo stared at him. Canlis stared at me. It was obvious she thought I had misread the facts of the case.

McKenzie turned out to be that blessing among witnesses, unflappable and concise. He answered my questions easily and simply about what had happened to him on the night of January 29, 1982. He pointed out Montalvo as the woman who stole the ring off his hand. Canlis now stared at Montalvo.

Hess cross-examined McKenzie, concentrating on the drinking, the small amount of property taken. When he was finished, he gave Montalvo a little smile. She nodded, blinked, frowned. McKenzie stepped off the stand, much more confidently.

"I have no further witnesses," I told Canlis.

"In view of this evidence, I'd like the court to deem this case a misdemeanor instead of sending it to Superior Court," Hess said.

He waited, pen over his file. I crossed my fingers mentally.

Canlis swept her penetrating, hard gaze over Montalvo and Hess. "No, I'm going to hold the defendant to answer to the charge in the complaint," she said.

That was a victory, I thought.

But Judge Canlis went on, "I'm also going to hold her to answer for violations of sections 211 and 470 based on what I heard this morning."

She had added charges of robbery and forgery. It carried a great deal of weight about the strength of the evidence when the judge did that. Hess and his client realized there was definite prison time involved.

Hess tried to reassure his irritated client as they got up and started walking out of the courtroom. The stout, black-dressed figure of Montalvo bustled to the courtroom's doors, unaware of the detectives waiting in the hallway for her.

Canlis called me to the bench as another prelim set up. "She's a monster," the judge said as Montalvo passed out the doors.

When I got into the hallway a few minutes later, Montalvo was in handcuffs, complaining, drawing a circle of fascinated people, obviously wondering what this harmless little old lady could have done to make these burly cops put her in handcuffs.

Montalvo was taken away. Hess was furious and turned on me. "That was chickenshit," he snapped angrily. "You should have told me."

"Then you would have had to tell her." It would have been Hess's ethical duty to inform Montalvo that she would be arrested. I didn't want to risk her escaping from the courtroom.

McKenzie waited, delighted at the scene. He was chipper and enthusiastic. "How'd I do?" he asked.

"You did exactly what we needed," I said. Both he and Canlis had given me much more leverage over Montalvo than I'd had going to court that morning.

I was busy trying to get more victims before a judge over the next few days, sorting out which of the cases against Montalvo could be re-filed.

Hess was also busy. After Montalvo had been in jail for several days on the new arrest, he managed to have a second judge release her on her own recognizance. I knew what must have persuaded the judge: *"Look at her, Your Honor. She's old. She has ties to the community. She's made all of her court appearances. The other cases against her have been dismissed."*

And one more official would have been fooled by Montalvo's act.

She went home to 1426 F Street on April 16, worried and desperate. She faced prison, and she couldn't deceive a judge if one of her victims actually testified.

Dorothea Montalvo needed enough money to get out of the country immediately. She couldn't pull her nurse routine now, though, because the agencies wouldn't use her.

Unfortunately, a source of easy cash was living with Montalvo at 1426 F Street. As I was working hard to resurrect the cases against her, Montalvo in the last weeks of April 1982 planned and carried out her first murder for profit.

15

I NEVER MET RUTH MUNROE, BUT SHE HAS HAUNTED ME FOR A decade. She was an utterly innocent victim of Dorothea Montalvo Puente. I have learned what happened to Ruth in her last weeks of life and it is as bad as anything one human being can do to another.

Ruth Munroe was a genial, pleasant woman in 1982, stocky, carrying her one hundred seventy-nine pounds on a five foot four inch frame. She wore glasses, had white hair, and occasionally put on a wig if she didn't feel like fixing her hair. She looked in many ways like Dorothea Montalvo. The difference was that Ruth actually had grandchildren, a family, a career. She was genuine, not an impostor.

Ruth had retired from the Gemco department store on Broadway and Riverside in Sacramento, after working as a clerk in the pharmacy for ten years. Oddly enough, Gemco was within a few yards of the cemetery where Bert Montoya would go, years later, and hear spirits calling to him from the grave.

Less than a year earlier, Ruth had married her second

husband, Harold Munroe. It was a periodically rough marriage. In late 1981 Harold was diagnosed with terminal cancer. They sold their home for about $20,000 and devoted the next few months to living as merrily as they wished, a last fling. They took a trip to Alturas, gambled and drank over a long weekend, and spent over $400. There were other trips, too. Ruth, never much of a drinker, now tried to keep up with her dying husband.

But he of course got worse, and they quarreled more often. Harold went into the Veterans Administration Hospital in Martinez in the early spring of 1982. Ruth remained upbeat, optimistic during this ordeal. She had just gone into a business partnership.

Harold had been drinking in various bars before he got too sick to go out. At the Flame Club he met Dorothea Montalvo, who was working there part-time as a cook and dishwasher. Harold, noting the similarity to his wife, brought Ruth along on a night out and introduced the two women.

Montalvo took the initiative and proposed that Ruth and she go into business as caterers. They would sell ready-made dishes to parties. "I've picked up a lot of business sense from the restaurants and bars I've worked at," Montalvo said.

The idea appealed to Ruth. She was down to only a few thousand dollars. The business would supplement her income, provide something to do as Harold became weaker and she needed a distraction.

Montalvo went to the owner of the Round Corner bar and bargained for use of the kitchen for about $150 a month. The bar's owner knew Harold well, and liked Ruth. She was a cheerful, hardworking, robust woman. Montalvo, with her sharp business sense, looked like an ideal partner.

Ruth then made a fatal mistake. To finance her share of the business, she withdrew money from her savings account. She and Montalvo, again at Dorothea's insistence, opened a joint bank account.

Ruth was proud of her new venture, certain it would be successful. Her only worry was Harold. He had started calling her from the hospital, querulous, bitter, and his continual depression made Ruth believe a divorce was inevitable. "You shouldn't be alone," Dorothea said helpfully. "I've got a lot of space where I live. We're in business together. Why shouldn't we share our living expenses, too?"

Dorothea must have used her most caring, sincere pose, because Ruth agreed, and on April 11, 1982, Easter Sunday, Ruth's three sons helped her move into 1426 F Street.

Ruth Munroe had a wide circle of close and old friends and four grown children, Allan, Houston, Bill, and Rosemary. Raised a Catholic, Ruth abhorred suicide and had a "fear of God," Allan said later.

Ruth threw herself into the new restaurant business. She worked long hours, cooking and washing up. Her children came by 1426 F Street to see her, talked to her on the phone, and found she was very happy and excited. She never mentioned any legal problems her partner was having, and apparently didn't even know about Dorothea's criminal background or her current crimes. Ruth, of course, never saw any of Dorothea's elderly victims around 1426 F Street.

If she had heard about Dorothea's legal pressure, Ruth probably would have tried to help her. Everyone who knew Ruth agreed she was a large-hearted, open woman. She always tried to help others. She trusted people.

During her last weeks, Ruth maintained her regular schedule of seeing friends and family. On April 14, she stopped by Nadine Nash's home. Nash, slight, with coppery-colored hair, had been like a sister to Ruth. It was natural to share good news with her.

Ruth had brought along a lot of money. It surprised Nash to see over $1,000 in Ruth's purse. "It was for the business," Nash remembered Ruth telling her. And Ruth was effusive about Dorothea, her partner. As an old friend, Nash sometimes called Ruth at 1426 F Street. She didn't know that the visit in mid-April would be the last time she saw Ruth. They had been close for over fifteen years.

Usually on Sundays, Ruth and her children got together or talked on the phone. She liked holding her grandchildren and hearing about their first steps or what they'd done. Her son Allan called Ruth on Sunday, April 25, to talk about her grandchildren, and she was as interested as she'd ever been. She didn't tell Allan, though, how poorly she felt.

But Ruth had told an old friend, Carmella "Camy" Lombardo about her terrors on April 24. The two women had worked at Gemco together in the pharmacy. Since Munroe retired, the two only saw each other about once a week, usually at the Tallac Village Beauty Salon where they both got their hair done.

Lombardo was shocked at Ruth's appearance. She was dazed, frightened, very worn. She seemed to be confused. They talked briefly about Harold's illness, and Lombardo offered to drive Ruth to Martinez. "No, Mrs. Puente can take me," Ruth answered.

Then, around someone she had known for years, Ruth broke down. Lombardo had trouble connecting the terrified, sick looking woman with her Gemco friend. Ruth said, almost in tears, "I can't talk to you. I think I'm going to die."

Lombardo was frightened now, too. "You've got to go to an emergency room or see a doctor," she said.

"I can't. I can't do anything," Ruth said, in terror. "I don't remember what I'm doing. I don't remember eating dinner or going to bed. I don't know where I am."

This was not the Ruth Munroe whom Lombardo had seen two or three weeks before. Something awful had happened and Ruth couldn't understand what it was. She said again that she thought she would die.

When she watched Ruth stagger out of the beauty parlor, Lombardo assumed she was going home, to bed. Camy Lombardo did not know that Ruth was living at 1426 F Street, alone, with Dorothea.

* * *

On the last night of her life, April 27, 1982, Ruth Munroe was visited by two of her children. Rosemary, called Rosie, came by early in the evening. She found her mother upstairs, in a deep, unrousable sleep. It was very unusual for Ruth to sleep so heavily. Rosie asked Dorothea, who hovered in the downstairs living room, what was wrong with Ruth.

"The doctor at the emergency room just gave your mother a shot," Dorothea said. "To calm her down."

"What emergency room?"

"At Davis Medical Center," Dorothea said.

Worried, but reassured by Dorothea's soothing calm and concern, Rosie went home. Ever since she met Dorothea, Rosie, like the rest of the family, had been impressed by her care for Ruth, her almost motherly worrying and fussing over her new roommate. Besides, Rosie felt better knowing that Dorothea was a nurse who had been trained to care for ill people. Ruth was certainly, Rosie believed, in good hands.

Sometime later in the evening, Bill Clausen stopped by after work. He was quite anxious about his mother's sudden health problems. In the last few years the two of them had grown very close.

Bill was brown-haired, with a dark mustache, medium sized and sometimes intense. Everything had seemed fine with his mother and Dorothea, living contentedly at 1426 F Street, until about three days earlier.

On April 24, Bill came by after work. He found Ruth sitting in the living room, propped up in a chair. He noticed his mother was drinking something. "What's that?" he asked.

"Dorothea fixed me a drink to calm me down," Ruth said. She was agitated. Harold had been calling. In fact, as Bill and she chatted, the phone rang. Bill answered it. It was Harold, complaining, angry, wanting to bother his wife again. Bill told him to stop calling.

Ruth went on drinking. Bill, unlike Rosie, was unaware his mother drank alcohol. He was also unaware of the bar-hopping weekends Harold and Ruth had taken in the last six or seven months. So he was startled when his mother told him the green, minty-smelling stuff she was sipping was crème de menthe.

For the next two nights when he came by, Ruth was sitting up, more stuporous each night, drinking a crème de menthe cocktail made by her friend Dorothea.

On April 27, Bill was met by Dorothea who invited him in. She wanted to brace him. "The doctor's just been here and given your mother a shot," Dorothea said.

"Why?" Bill asked quickly.

"She was very upset and nervous."

"I better see her." Bill noticed that Ruth wasn't sitting in the living room. She must be upstairs in her bedroom.

"I don't think you should go up there," Dorothea said, her hands clasped. "She's sleeping. You shouldn't disturb her now."

For the first time, Bill disregarded Dorothea's professional nursing advice and went upstairs to see his mother for himself. He found her in bed, facing the wall, on her side. Her eyes were open. She didn't appear to notice him. He gently shook her. She didn't respond. She seemed drugged, just as Dorothea said.

"Don't worry, Mom," Bill said softly, leaning to her. "Everything's going to be all right. Dorothea will take care of you."

He was anxious when a tear came out of his mother's eye. "I'll come back soon," he said. He left the bedroom, and on his way out of 1426 F, Dorothea, patting him, comforting him, said that all Ruth needed was some rest. "I'll be here to look after her," Dorothea said, closing the front door.

Nadine Nash called that evening, hoping to talk to Ruth.

"She can't come to the phone," Dorothea said.

"Why not?"

"The doctor's been here and given her a shot. She's sleeping."

"Tell her I hope she feels better." Nash hung up, a feeling of unease troubling her.

* * *

Rosie was jolted awake by a ringing phone around 5:30 A.M. April 28.

It was Dorothea. "Something's wrong with your mother. I've called the paramedics. You better come over."

Rosie jumped from bed, dressing hastily in the pre-dawn. She called Ruth's other children.

When she hurried into 1426 F Street, Rosie noticed the police squad car, the emergency vehicles parked on the dark street, curious neighbors standing on the sidewalk.

A tearful, anguished Dorothea met her in the living room. "Your mother died," she said.

Officer Robert Nichols, a patrol cop, was first on the scene. He got to 1426 F around 6:00 A.M. in response to a casualty call. When he arrived, he was met by Dorothea Montalvo. He started making notes about what had happened. "She was all right around four this morning," Dorothea told Nichols. "I checked on her. Then about forty minutes ago she wouldn't wake up so I called the fire department."

Nichols said he wanted to see the deceased person himself. As he walked upstairs, Dorothea told him that Ruth Munroe had a heart condition and she was suffering great emotional stress lately because of divorce proceedings against her husband.

Nichols went to the upstairs side bedroom. He quickly determined that the pink nightgown–clad woman in the bed was indeed dead. He came back downstairs and called the coroner and his supervisor.

Within a few minutes, more people appeared, frantic and crying family members of the dead woman. They stayed in the living room, talking to Nichols or to Dorothea, who tried to comfort them. Dorothea told Bill and Rosie she had gone to see Ruth around four, and given her a drink of grapefruit juice and water. But she mentioned to others that she gave Ruth an injection. It did not sound strange, given Dorothea's nursing background.

The house was brightly lit up, filled with grieving people,

men in uniform, as the sun started coming up. The coroner's assistant arrived to remove Ruth's body. He also talked with the tired but firm Dorothea. "She was having pains in the left side of her arm," Dorothea told the coroner, with a medical person's specificity.

The coroner went to the bedroom. He made a point of looking for unusual items in the room. Dorothea plainly believed the woman had died from a heart attack, and yet subtly suggested she might have killed herself. On a table near the bed the coroner found a prescription bottle of Miltown, a tranquilizer, for Ruth Munroe. He did not find any other bottles or medications in the room. Nor did he find any suicide note.

Rosie, Bill, and other members of the family could not believe Ruth was dead. They wept with Dorothea. Since Ruth had no known serious medical problems, Dorothea's suggestion that perhaps suicide was the explanation for this sudden, horrific death, fitted what the family saw at the house. Perhaps Ruth had been more anguished over her divorce than they had realized.

Knowing nothing of Dorothea's legal problems or Mildred Ballenger's efforts, the monstrous idea that someone had deliberately, cold-bloodedly drugged and then poisoned Ruth Munroe for money never entered their minds on April 28, 1982.

Looking at the sad, sympathetic, grandmotherly face of Dorothea that terrible morning, how could they have suspected murder?

Ruth's body was taken downtown to the coroner's office. Since her death was from an undetermined cause in a home, without any physician present, an autopsy was mandatory.

Later on April 28, a pathologist examined the body of the sixty-one-year-old woman and found no visible external trauma. Even after Munroe's body was cut open, Dr. Gwen Hall saw nothing to explain sudden death, although Ruth's liver was enlarged, and she had a slightly enlarged heart and mild hardening of the arteries.

But the liver bothered Dr. Hall as she examined it. There had been fatty damage to the liver, the kind associated with either alcoholism or chemical toxicity. This might be significant. Dr. Hall took tissue samples from the liver, stomach, and kidneys.

When she opened Ruth's stomach, Dr. Hall discovered a dark green mint-smelling material. There was no evidence the dead woman had eaten any solid food for several days. Dr. Hall had found the remnants of Ruth's crème de menthe cocktails.

Dr. Hall reviewed Ruth's medical history through the records of her family doctor. She had seen him often for cold-type symptoms. In January he prescribed meprobamate or Miltown for the anxiety Ruth was feeling. Other than that, she had been a healthy woman when she saw her doctor last on March 26.

Dr. Hall packaged up the tissue and blood samples and sent them to a toxicologist for analysis. The results came back within two weeks. Ruth Munroe's blood and stomach contents showed she had died from a massive overdose of acetaminophen and codeine, in other words, Tylenol and codeine. There was also a high but prescription level amount of Miltown in her system. She had not had a heart attack.

It was, Dr. Hall realized, a puzzle. Miltown and the gram-amounts of Tylenol and codeine would suppress breathing. The Tylenol and codeine alone were sufficient to kill. None was found in her bedroom.

The coroner's office classified Ruth's death as being of "undeterminate cause." Suicide was not ruled out, but nothing else, including homicide, fitted the clinical evidence. There simply wasn't enough information to rule the death anything at all.

A melancholy, shocked family got together at Allan's house on April 30. The unthinkable had happened, and they were still trying to grasp it.

Rosie's husband, John, was there. Tall, black-haired, and

intelligent, John did not share Ruth's children's high opinion of Dorothea Montalvo. There was something wrong with that woman, a skewed aspect to the caring grandmother he couldn't quite put his finger on.

Rosie said they had to accept the real possibility that Ruth had killed herself. "She didn't want to get old," Rosie said sadly.

Out of the blue, Houston's girlfriend blurted out, "I think Dorothea Montalvo killed her."

John then had an epiphany, his suspicions and disquiet coming together in an angry burst. "I believe the same thing," he said suddenly.

But neither Bill nor Rosie, Allan, or Houston could face that horrific, almost unimaginable possibility.

John intended to see where the evidence went. He worked on Rosie, and gradually she came around to his thinking. She called UCDMC and found out that Ruth had never been to the emergency room there on April 27 or any other day. No doctor had come to 1426 F either. Dorothea was lying.

John got in touch with the DA's office on May 1. A receptionist told him to talk to the police if he had a possible murder to report. So John called SPD Homicide and was connected to Sergeant Dave Schwartz. "What you've got to do first is get everyone to write down a statement of what happened," Schwartz told John.

Wasting no time, John went back to Ruth's other children and had them recount, on paper, everything they had seen or heard over the last few days. He turned the statements over to Schwartz, but after reading them, the detective wasn't encouraging. "Unless you saw Dorothea Montalvo give this woman a lethal drug or she told you she did that, there's not much I can do."

"You mean there's not enough evidence?" John asked incredulously.

"There's no case here at this point."

John was furious. He had become Ruth's champion. He said to Rosie, "I'm going over there and I'm going to kill her," meaning Dorothea. He did angrily confront Dorothea at 1426 F, but did nothing else.

The police reaction to the facts strengthened Bill and Rosie's judgment that their mother had killed herself.

Several weeks later, Bill went to 1426 F Street and gathered up his mother's clothes. He talked to Dorothea briefly, the two of them commiserating over the loss of a sweet woman.

It was a tragedy that Ruth's family determined to put behind them.

They did not realize that the money Ruth had drawn out for her business with Dorothea had vanished. The joint bank account was emptied as well. In early May, with a date in Superior Court to answer robbery, forgery, and grand theft charges racing toward her, Dorothea bought a plane ticket for Mexico.

The unanswered mystery remains, though. Why did she not leave Sacramento as soon as she had what she wanted? Instead, she acted as if she hoped to be caught.

16

"I'M DRUNK," DOROTHEA SAID, SLURRING HER WORDS. "Everything's going wrong. Everybody's taking advantage of me. You've got to come over."

Dorothy Osborne listened to the worried, clearly drunken woman on the other end of the telephone. Osborne, forty-nine, had known Dorothea Montalvo for about a year, and had been cared for by her. It was midmorning, May 16, 1982. "Well, I don't really want to go out, Dorothea," Osborne said.

"You've got to come over. We can have a few drinks, talk about life. Things haven't been going well." Pause. "A woman died."

"I'm sorry about that. But I can't come to your house."

Dorothea, anxious, muttering said, "All right, all right. I'll come to you. I've got to see someone."

It was a strange call, unlike any other Osborne had gotten from Dorothea. She waited, wondering what was so upsetting the usually calm, almost cold Dorothea Montalvo.

* * *

Osborne lived at 1620 G Street in apartment 10, only a few blocks from 1426 F. It took Dorothea only a short while to show up around eleven. Osborne had been thinking. Who had died? What woman? Dorothea had never mentioned a death that disturbed her.

Dorothea came to see Osborne dressed plainly, in a simple solid-colored dress, her hair pulled back. She brought over a bottle of Korbel brandy and some vodka.

"I'll make some drinks and we can talk," Dorothea said. "I've got a lot on my mind."

Osborne followed her into the kitchen. Dorothea opened cabinets, got out grenadine, grapefruit juice, apple and cranapple juice. "No, no," she hustled Osborne out, "you go watch TV. I'll bring everything in."

While Osborne sat in the living room, Dorothea worked alone in the kitchen, finally coming in with a large glass of the peculiar cocktail she had mixed. Osborne didn't like the biting, strong taste. "It's very sharp," she said, complaining.

"It's good," Dorothea said.

"Why don't you have some?"

"I only want vodka right now," Dorothea said, sipping from her own glass of straight vodka.

Dorothea launched into a monologue. She didn't say anything specifically about the mysterious death, but wailed and complained that people were lying about her, using her, putting terrible pressure on her. Osborne listened, finished her drink, and left Dorothea briefly to go to a nearby liquor store for something other than the brandy or vodka. She drank a little more, switched to iced tea to get the persistent sour, stinging taste of the first cocktail out of her mouth.

Dorothea never stopped complaining. She paced the living room, then sat down opposite Osborne, moaning about the wretched way she was being abused.

It was a little after noon and Osborne, listening to the incessant voice sitting near her, suddenly began to grow hazy, dim. The last thing she heard was Dorothea, whining. Then she passed out.

It was twilight outside when Osborne came to again. She

staggered around the apartment, trying to wake up. It was then she noticed that some of her checks were gone, and her credit cards, and six rolls of pennies with her name and phone number on them.

Osborne intuitively realized there was something wrong with the drink Dorothea had made for her. That weird mixture of juices and liquors could hide any strange taste. Osborne got into the kitchen, and found some of the reddish liquid remaining in a blender. She scooped it into an empty pill bottle, along with a white powder she noticed. She called the police at once.

When the police arrived, Osborne explained what had happened, who had done this to her, and gave them the pill bottle of liquid and white powder.

"She said she's going to Mexico," Osborne alerted the police. "Dorothea told me she's already got the tickets."

When Dorothea Montalvo was arrested on May 19, she still had Osborne's credit cards and rolled pennies with her. She also had the damning plane tickets.

She was taken downtown to jail, and denied bail. No judge would let her out again. She had committed a crime while on bail for another offense, and she had obviously made plans to flee the country. Dorothea Montalvo would stay in jail until her case was in Superior Court for trial.

I was delighted when the reports and files came to me. At last someone had caught Montalvo in possession of a drug. Osborne's physical effects were identical to McKenzie, Gosling, Gregory, Chalmers, and Maleville. So was the reason for drugging: theft.

I sent the pill bottle and powder over to the Crime Lab for analysis. My theory, based on the symptoms the victims experienced, was that Montalvo had used chloral hydrate, called a "Mickey Finn."

It was a terrific disappointment when the results came back. There was no controlled substance in either the reddish liquid or powder. But I found out years later that the

Crime Lab in 1982 was comparatively primitive. It could not, in fact, detect chloral hydrate or a whole range of barbiturate/tranquilizing drugs. Nor could they test for flurazepam, the generic name of Dalmane, which had been stolen from Irene Gregory.

Montalvo and I appeared before a judge later in May. She looked different, an orange jail sweatshirt giving her a sporty look. She pleaded with the judge that she had not been planning any escape, only going to visit relatives in Mexico. She would definitely be in Sacramento on the day of her Superior Court arraignment on the other charges.

I only pointed out the obvious—a plane ticket, another crime—and argued that the defendant should stay in jail to ensure the community's safety and her presence in court. The judge agreed.

Hoping for the best, I went ahead and re-filed Gosling, Gregory and added Osborne. I wanted Montalvo and her lawyer to face as many charges as possible in Superior Court and perhaps realize that a plea was preferable to a trial.

By early June, though, negotiations with Hess were going nowhere. I had not, however, heard of the terrible events at 1426 F Street on April 28. Ruth Munroe's death would have instantly resolved the question of what to do with Dorothea Montalvo.

There were a few problems. The DA's office was in convulsions in June, throwing out the incumbent, and electing a new District Attorney. I was going to debates, moderating events, acting as impartial arbiter between the two candidates because they knew I'd be gone in a few months.

Frawley and I had been working out what to do with Montalvo once things calmed down in the DA's office. The objectives were simple. First, get as much time in prison as possible, to keep her away from more victims. Second, have her plead to enough separate crimes so her rap sheet, her criminal record, reflected what she had done. As Mildred

Ballenger impressed on me, Montalvo had gotten away for so long with so much largely because her rap sheet only faintly suggested her true criminality.

To help speed this plea bargaining along, I filed a charge, section 222 of the penal code, citing Dorothy Osborne as the victim. That felony was known as "administering a stupefying agent for the purpose of committing a second felony," robbery or theft. I didn't know what drug Montalvo had used, but she certainly had drugged her victims. She would have to plead to the 222 to have it on her record for the future.

The major problem, though, was that Hess thought Montalvo should get a much better deal. I had offered him three felonies involving Osborne, Gregory, and McKenzie. In return, Montalvo would have no other charges filed against her, based on what the DA's office knew at that time, and she would serve about four years in prison.

"She's helping the cops," Hess told me. We were in Superior Court, Department Four, waiting for Judge Roger Warren. "Give her something more."

We had been going back and forth with offers for weeks. This latest development threatened everything. I still had shaky victims and no solid proof of drugging, but I didn't want to make Montalvo happy.

I called the Sacramento police and got referred to Schwartz. "What's going on, Dave?" I asked. "Montalvo's lawyer says she's working for Vice."

He laughed. "Well, what's happening is that she's over in the Women's section in jail," which was miles from downtown Sacramento, isolated, "and the younger girls are coming to her with their problems. Boyfriend troubles, things they've done. She's kind of the mother confessor for these younger inmates."

"So what is she doing for you guys?"

"These girls are telling Montalvo about crimes they've committed, crimes their boyfriends did, and asking her advice."

"Montalvo wants to trade this information?" I asked. That sounded likely.

"Right. She'll give up these kids, whatever they told her, in return for a better deal on her cases."

Schwartz and I both laughed at Montalvo's limitless duplicity. "The stuff is no good," Schwartz said.

I told him Vice couldn't use her, either.

"We shouldn't give her anything," Schwartz said firmly.

I told Hess that while I still wanted to resolve all of Montalvo's cases at once, she wouldn't get a better offer. He nodded. He was, he said, getting out of representing her. He had too many other clients. A private lawyer would come in and take over.

It was extremely frustrating. Montalvo was balking at pleading to anything, trying to twist a deal all the time, and now I had to start all over with a new lawyer.

Montalvo's next lawyer was Dennis Porter, in his twenties, a nervous, uncertain man who smoked a lot. We met on June 25. He instantly repeated Hess's belief that Montalvo should get a break because she was helping the cops. In fact, he thought she should get immunity in return for turning over so many other defendants.

Porter didn't think he was going to have much client control, based on his initial meeting with Dorothea in jail.

We set another plea negotiation for July 13. I didn't want to string this out forever, especially if I had to go to trial. My victims didn't improve as time went on. I needed something strong to use against Montalvo.

I talked to Schwartz. I thought I could push Porter. "You better send over whatever you have on Montalvo's bad one-eighty-seven," I told Schwartz, using the penal code section for murder.

"Okay. You know it's no good. You can't use it in court."

"I don't want to use it in court. I want to have it handy."

Schwartz warned me there wasn't much. He sent over a one-page face sheet on Esther Busby's poisoning. It was, I saw, completely useless as a case, but very powerful as a bargaining chip to persuade Dorothea Montalvo to plead guilty to the other crimes.

The only defect in my reasoning was that Dorothea Montalvo had on her mind the murder of Ruth Munroe, not Esther Busby.

On the morning of July 13, 1982, Porter and I met in Department Four. We went to the sunlit hallway behind the courtroom so he could smoke. He had just been in the tank, the courthouse jail cells, to see Montalvo. "She doesn't want the deal," he said.

"I thought she was interested."

"She thinks she deserves immunity. I told her what you said, but she says she's helping the police, and I believe her." He squinted at me nervously. Montalvo was giving him strict marching orders.

I realized I had to push as hard as possible. "All right. Before we leave court," I said, "you should know that the Sacramento police think she's responsible for a homicide."

"Oh, Jesus," Porter sighed, his cigarette hanging from his hand.

I showed him the one-page Busby summary. He read it quietly.

"The offer now would be that she pleads to all four victims, four separate cases. I'll agree not to prosecute any other crimes known to my office now."

"Including this," he held the Busby summary page.

"Including that," I took the page from him. I sent him a copy of it the next day.

"I'll talk to her again," Porter said. He looked white and shaky.

We were back in court on July 14, the following day. "She'll take the deal," Porter said, after he came out of the tank. "And she agrees that the maximum time she can do is four years."

"Four years eight months in state prison. That's my recommendation to the judge."

We went back into Judge Warren's chambers and told him the proposed disposition. Warren was a younger judge, with no criminal trial experience, but he had good sense. He said he'd abide by this plea bargain unless he saw something very bizarre in Montalvo's probation report before sentencing. Then he'd reject the whole deal and we'd start over, ready to go to trial.

Porter stood beside Montalvo in the dock. Judge Warren went through the mechanics of gathering the re-filed cases into his courtroom, postponing the actual pleas until July 21. Montalvo whispered to Porter and answered hesitantly, with a nervous, wary stare at the judge or me whenever she was asked if she understood the proceedings. Judge Warren asked if she agreed to continue the trial status conference to the new date.

"Yes, sir, I do," Montalvo answered in her quavery, old lady's voice. I had never seen a more incongruous defendant in an orange jumpsuit than this timorous, bespectacled, old, white-haired woman.

Dorothea Montalvo's appearance, either in municipal court or in Judge Warren's courtroom, usually caused a murmur of astonishment among the spectators. It was always difficult to reconcile the white-haired woman with what she was charged with having done.

On July 21, Porter and I were back in Department Four. I crossed my fingers and hoped Montalvo hadn't grown stubborn again and decided to throw the plea bargain out.

Porter and I spent some time back in chambers with Judge Warren, explaining the plea bargain. I told him my reasons for it were simple: I had sick victims, and this arrangement gave the sentencing judge enough latitude to put Montalvo in prison for a long time. I didn't want Judge Warren to state in open court, though, that the DA was forgoing prosecution in a homicide in order to get these pleas from Montalvo. The less I had to explain about

Busby's case and the police assessment that it was unprovable, the better.

If Montalvo heard me say that I wouldn't pursue her on a homicide, Judge Warren would probably ask, in front her, why I was doing so. I knew if Montalvo heard me say how bad the Busby case was, she'd insist on going to trial, having also heard that her living victims were too sick to come to court.

It was a delicate hide-and-seek game when we got into open court. Judge Warren, dubious about it all, agreed not to mention the homicide in any fashion.

The courtroom was nearly empty. Montalvo and Porter seated themselves at the counsel table. We began when the judge asked Montalvo a series of required questions.

"Do you understand the crimes with which you've been charged, in other words, the nature of the charges against you?"

She glanced at Porter who nodded. "Yes," she answered.

"Have you discussed the charges, your possible defenses, and this suggested disposition with your lawyer?"

Another glance at a nodding Porter. "Yes," Montalvo said, her hands clasped in front of her.

Every so often, Montalvo would look over at me. Her mouth was set. She had an inscrutable, but cold look behind her glasses. I was not one of her favorite people.

I gave a factual basis for each plea and then Judge Warren, a careful man, asked her four separate times if she was pleading guilty knowingly to each charge. Four times Montalvo said she was. She pled guilty to drugging Osborne on May 16 in order to steal from her.

The judge then put on the record that no other crimes known to the District Attorney would be prosecuted. Montalvo nodded solemnly.

Leaving the courtroom after she was taken back to a holding cell, I told Porter he had done the right thing, tying all her cases into one deal. I felt satisfied. I had gotten all four victims some justice and had used an unprosecutable suspicious death as a bargaining lever. Dorothea Montalvo would be off the streets for years.

Judge Warren set the sentencing for August 18. I thought, as I walked away from Porter out of the courthouse, I had accomplished a lot.

In fact, the white-haired, nervous old lady had out-smarted me.

The local press started picking up on Montalvo. Her grandmotherly exterior and the nasty nature of her crimes were irresistible during a slow news summer.

In a front page story on July 22, the *Sacramento Bee*, the area's largest daily, jokingly wrote that Montalvo had robbed "an elderly chap" in a bar after slipping him a Mickey Finn. I made the mistake of adding to the light-hearted spirit of the coverage by saying that Montalvo was "the most mild, pleasant appearing grandmother you could possibly think of. But I wouldn't sit down and have a drink with her."

I called her "the quintessential granny." Six years later I would cringe in disgust, seeing that stupid remark repeated as the *Bee* reported on the first bodies dug up at 1426 F Street.

The TV stories were also hitting the comical aspect of a larcenous old lady.

But I didn't treat Montalvo lightly when I got back to my office. Her files were going to the county Probation Office for the preparation of a pre-sentence report. This report would guide Judge Warren in making his sentence or rejecting the plea bargain. I wanted him to follow the plea bargain, but be starkly aware of how dangerous and malign Montalvo was.

It is unethical for a DA to send letters or call a probation officer without letting defense counsel know about it. The defense then has a chance to offer any opposing arguments.

But in difficult cases, or especially vicious and unusual situations, the normal practice was to write a detailed file memo that included every statement the DA intended to make before the judge. The memo also highlighted parts of the file, so the probation officer could go right to the heart of the crimes.

Ballenger and Schwartz had sensitized me to Montalvo's slippery abilities and I didn't want her fooling the probation officer.

I wrote a lengthy file memo, hoping to influence how the probation officer wrote his report for Judge Warren. My major point was to stress how Montalvo preyed on the most vulnerable and helpless members of the community.

When the report itself came back weeks later, I was pleasantly surprised to see how much Montalvo had cooperated in making herself look bad.

I showed Frawley the probation report Tony Ruiz had prepared. We agreed that he had caught on early to many of Montalvo's tricks. For example, he wrote that although she made remorseful comments during the interview, "in this officer's opinion her expression of remorse was diluted by her attempts to manipulate the interview."

She was pretty blatant, too:

> While this officer was explaining the purpose of the interview, the defendant, after noting this writer's Hispanic surname, interrupted to explain that she, too, was of Hispanic descent. Further, although the defendant appeared distraught and tearful throughout the interview, it was apparent to this writer that she was extremely observant of the notes that were being made during the interview and, at one point, asked for an explanation of a particular word this writer had written in his notes. The defendant attempted to read, upside down, the officer's notes, as she sat on the opposite side of the interview booth.

Then Montalvo gave her version of the crimes she had committed. She felt badly, she told Ruiz, that the victims had lost some of their possessions. "She could see they were needy people or had a right to continue to possess their property. She indicated that she, too, had suffered as a child and disliked seeing other individuals suffer likewise."

But as far as admitting doing much of anything, Montalvo tried to have it both ways, being caught and innocent at the same time. She denied taking anything from Dorothy Gosling, although she agreed she had forged the woman's checks. "She was quick to point out that she made restitution, but she could not reasonably explain her actions as she reportedly did not need the money that bad."

Nor could Montalvo admit doing much to Irene Gregory. "She was confused as to her actions in this offense," Ruiz wrote, "but she nevertheless denied that she had ever been in the victim's apartment and denied taking any items from her. She indicated she had only seen this victim at the beauty shop they both patronized."

Frawley and I had wondered how Montalvo would explain away the Osborne drugging. First denying everything, Montalvo told the probation officer that she "admitted administering a drug but could not recall what it was composed of. After first indicating she had no explanation for her behavior, she then changed her story and denied administering any drug at all." Osborne, Montalvo said, invited her over to drink and gave her the wrapped pennies to buy beer.

What about Malcolm McKenzie's encounter with Montalvo in the bar? She claimed now she had only taken and forged two checks. She never took his coins or ring. "However," as Ruiz wrote again and again in the report, "she could not explain her actions."

Montalvo told Ruiz that "she pled to certain counts made against her as it was simply part of the plea bargain arrangements."

In other words, she lied to Judge Warren throughout the taking of those pleas when he asked her direct questions.

There was nothing in the report about Esther Busby, nor did Montalvo bring up the death of Ruth Munroe.

"She doesn't like to admit anything," Frawley said, with

characteristic understatement, when he gave me back the report.

I was back in front of Judge Warren on August 18. Porter was unhappy, and so was Montalvo, who muttered and shook her head as she sat at the counsel table.

She was annoyed because Warren had informed Porter and me that he found Montalvo so bad, he intended to give her the maximum possible sentence based on the four charges—five years in state prison. Ruiz had called her "callous and unconscionable" in what she did, and Judge Warren emphatically agreed.

Warren asked Porter for his thoughts. Porter argued that the judge should pick a shorter prison term. Warren was firm. Either he would give her five years or the whole plea bargain would be set aside. Neither Porter nor I wanted that.

I didn't know that Montalvo had written two letters to the judge, trying to influence his opinion of her. On June 8 she told him, "I admit I'm a forger," then said she had been a civic figure, made many charitable contributions, helped worthy political candidates with "clean money," and was burdened with a rough early life.

She wrote again on July 25, apparently sensing that the young judge wasn't so pliable as she assumed and her efforts to manipulate Tony Ruiz had failed. Montalvo told Warren that the plane tickets found on her were so she could take care of her dead sister's needy family in Mexico. No sister, of course, had died. Montalvo hoped the judge would give her the shortest possible prison time so she could help her family in Mexico by sending them "money to buy meat, eggs, milk." Her surviving brothers, she said, were too old to provide for the family.

"I don't mind if I have to report each day or what," Montalvo offered helpfully.

"I know I have done wrong," she went on. "These months in jail have been terrible on me. But worse on my family, as I have not been able to send them any money. I feel so terrible for the poor people I did wrong to."

Judge Warren, however new he was to criminal trials, was no fool. He had read the probation report's detailed summaries of what Montalvo had done and he knew that lurking in the background was something worse, even if the DA couldn't prosecute it.

He sat on the bench, spoke calmly, directly, shortly to the frowning Montalvo in front of him. He sentenced her to five years in state prison, with credit for the few months she had already been in county jail. "Do you understand the sentence?" he asked her.

"I do," Montalvo nodded sulkily.

The bailiff escorted her back through the clerk's office, down to the second floor holding cell, and then she was processed and put on a state bus and sent to the California Institution for Women in Frontera to do her time.

I left the courtroom assuming I would never see Porter or Dorothea Montalvo again. I got back to my office, called Dave Schwartz to tell him the sentence and to pass along the good news to Mildred Ballenger. We could all breathe a little easier.

On August 19, 1982, the *Bee* ran another big story on the thieving grandmother. It was more sober than the earlier stories. The headline was: "Woman Who Slipped Mickeys Draws Five Years." She was described as being handcuffed, calm, wearing a yellow jail T-shirt when sentenced.

It looked like a nice windup to the case of Dorothea Montalvo.

On August 20, 1982, I got a phone call in the afternoon. "We just read your name in the newspaper," the unknown man said. "About Dorothea and her sentencing. We think she poisoned our mother."

17

WHAT HAD HAPPENED? I WONDERED, SHOCKED BY THAT CALL. I thought I knew everything about Dorothea Montalvo's criminality, but she had kept the worst secret to herself.

It was Bill Clausen who called me and I asked him to come down to the office immediately.

That afternoon, with his brother Allan and sister Rosie, I met for the first time with Ruth Munroe's children. They sat in a semicircle in my small office and told me everything that had led up to April 28 and their mother's death.

Bill did most of the talking. He had the *Bee* article with him that had pointed them to me.

"What killed her," Bill said intently, "was a lot of codeine. The combination of pills. That's her husband's medicine, it wasn't hers. There was a lot stronger stuff around the house if she was going to kill herself." Until they saw the story about Dorothea's other crimes that spring, they believed she was a kindly, caring woman, trusted by Ruth Munroe completely. Ruth's children didn't stop bitterly blaming themselves for listening to Dorothea the whole time they were with me.

When we finished that afternoon, I was deadened and self blaming too, realizing Dorothea had fooled me as well.

I shook hands with Bill, Allan, and Rosie, and agreed to meet again early the next week. I wanted to see any documentary evidence they had, like bank statements, notes, or reports. I asked them to bring Ruth Munroe's death certificate.

As soon as they were gone, I muttered about their revelations to everyone in Team Four. What a disaster.

I talked to Frawley, O'Mara, and a bureau chief, telling them what had just happened. I went back through the Montalvo files, trying to see if Ruth Munroe's name was mentioned anywhere. It was critical for two reasons. First, I couldn't prosecute Dorothea for the murder if the DA's office had known about it before the plea bargain on July 21. And second, I needed to reassure myself I hadn't let a horrible murder slip through my hands.

But there was nothing in the files on Ruth Munroe from the police. I took a mental deep breath of partial relief and wrote a memo to O'Mara, as head of Major Crimes, alerting him to the Clausens' allegations.

Then on August 22, I called Schwartz at SPD.

I only had a little over a week left in the DA's office. My temporary job was ending before Labor Day. The investigation of Ruth Munroe's murder had to be started before I left. I owed the family that much.

The Clausens came back on August 30, bringing the death certificate. Rosie had some additional information, too. In March Munroe had lent Montalvo $600 secured by two rings. Montalvo took the rings back when she claimed she was going to see a sick relative. Munroe was never repaid. It occurred to me suddenly that the rings might belong to either Malcolm McKenzie or Irene Gregory. Montalvo didn't want stolen property in someone else's possession and so got them back from Munroe as soon as she could.

Telling me about Ruth's last days was terrible. Rosie broke down and wept.

"Dorothea told us," Bill said, pointing to himself and Rosie, "that Mom was having a nervous breakdown. She said a doctor had just come out and given her a shot, and that's why she wasn't awake or wouldn't talk to us."

Dorothea had told the patrol officer and assistant coroner that Ruth was having heart problems and had suffered a heart attack. Dorothea would say whatever it took to throw the listener's attention away from her.

It was another grueling, tense meeting. At its end, all I could do was to promise Bill and Rosie that I would make sure their information got to the police and Major Crimes.

Finally, after years as a prosecutor, I realized there isn't much you can really do for the survivors. Evil, when it hits a family, leaves an ineradicable injury.

The only bright spot I saw was that Ruth Munroe's killer was behind bars and would stay there for years. It might just be possible to get some justice for the family and Ruth. Montalvo could be charged with murder.

I typed out more memos for Schwartz and O'Mara, including the death certificate. Frawley and I talked about the best way to proceed, and putting it all in the hands of Schwartz and Major Crimes in our office was the best path to follow. I talked to O'Mara, and he agreed to check out the Clausens' information.

It turned out that my meeting with the Clausens was the last one I had as a deputy district attorney. I had to clean out my desk by September 1.

O'Mara put a seasoned investigator in Major Crimes on the case. He also got in touch with Schwartz, reviewing the statements the family had made in early May. It looked like suicide, given the divorce, Harold's illness, the lack of more evidence about Ruth Munroe's final hours, was as likely a possibility as murder. When the DA's investigator submitted his report several months later, corroborating suicide and relegating Munroe and Montalvo's connection to coincidence, O'Mara concluded that even if he did file a murder charge, he was not likely to get a conviction.

It was better, all around, to drop the matter, secure in the knowledge Dorothea Montalvo was in prison.

The story of Ruth Munroe's ugly murder sank away into limbo until 1988 when more bodies were brought up from 1426 F Street and the whole heartless past of Dorothea Montalvo, then called Puente, would be exposed to view once again.

PART 4

18

When Charles Willgues finished talking with Donna Johansson on the phone on Wednesday night, November 16, 1988, he was not alone in his apartment. He had a newsman from a local TV station with him.

All into the remainder of that afternoon and early evening, Willgues had been trying to recall where he had seen Donna before. It was not her name that tickled his memory, but her features, the white hair, glasses, the penetrating dark eyes and set mouth. "I know this woman," he thought. "I've seen her before."

Was it on TV? Around seven-thirty that night, Willgues remembered seeing Donna on the TV that morning. He called KCBS-TV and talked to the assignment editor. He described Donna and her interest in his benefit payments, his living alone. The newsman, Gene Silver, came to Willgues's apartment a little later, bringing a newspaper with a photo in it of the fugitive Dorothea Puente.

More than interest in a great story drew Silver to Willgues. "This woman could have been trying to prey on him," Silver said later. "He was disabled and drawing a pension." A prime target. Silver thought Willgues was in real danger.

The two men talked for an hour, going over what Puente said, how she acted, what she said about her plans. Willgues told Silver about the Thursday date and the tentative plans for Puente to cook Thanksgiving dinner. The two men realized how close Willgues had just come to heading down the same road with Puente others had traveled.

Willgues was fairly sure, after he saw the newspaper photo, that Donna Johansson and Dorothea Puente were the same person. He and Silver watched the 9:00 P.M. news on KCBS and again saw a photo of Puente. Willgues had no doubt now about who he had been drinking with. He called her at the Royal Viking, making sure she was in her room.

It was time, Willgues and Silver agreed, to call the police.

Puente, after the call from Willgues, had stuck to her routine of the last few days and stayed in room 31 at night. Perhaps she really felt unsafe around Third and Alvarado after dark. If so, it was an enormous irony, given her murderous propensities.

She passed the time watching TV, dozing, reading the newspapers scattered over the bureau.

After 11:00 P.M. there was a flurry of hard knocks on the door. Puente opened it. Several detectives and police officers from LAPD came in quickly, using her real name.

"I'll go with you," she said, almost meekly. In her purse the detectives found her driver's license. They had her picture from Frontera in 1982. They knew who she was. For the first time, Puente was arrested, handcuffed, and in custody for murder.

Shortly after midnight, Wednesday blending into Thursday in the city's darkness, Puente was driven in a small caravan of police cars to the Rampart Division station. She had said very little getting ready at the motel room or sitting in the squad car. She wore her red overcoat and scarlet pumps. Her white hair straggled somewhat, and when she was put into a cell, she was bowed and tired. "She's very quiet and peaceful," a police sergeant told the crowd of reporters at the station, "looking at the floor, and has her head down."

There was a burst of calls back and forth to Parker Center, the headquarters of the Los Angeles police. The decision was made not to question Puente. The LAPD was fearful that haste might jeopardize any admissions Puente made. She was, of course, rightfully a Sacramento prisoner and needed to be returned to the capital as soon as possible. There is a local jurisdictional rule in Los Angeles that suspects arrested within city limits must be arraigned on charges within five hours. Puente would have to be in court by Thursday morning.

LAPD fervently wanted to get her out of the city and back to Sacramento to avoid any future legal problems if she was arraigned in one city, then re-arraigned in the capital.

In Sacramento, Chief Kearns held a brief press conference, at last able to announce good news in the case. He was happy she had been captured. As he spoke, John Cabrera was already making arrangements to bring Puente back for trial.

Cabrera discovered that a regular charter from Sacramento to Los Angeles couldn't be set up until later Thursday morning. By that time, Puente would have been tangled up in the Los Angeles courts. There was, though, an unorthodox transportation method available, and he got permission from his superiors to use it.

Cabrera didn't know he was setting himself and the police up for as much criticism as they had gotten by letting Puente get away on Saturday.

Sacramento's NBC-TV affiliate, KCRA, was prepared to fly a cameraman and reporter Mike Boyd south as soon as Puente was arrested. Boyd wanted to get pictures of the places she had visited, the motel, Monte Carlo I, the T.G. Express. A photographer from the *Bee* would also be on the chartered plane.

Boyd and KCRA offered space on the Learjet to the police if, as Puente was flown back, they could take pictures of her. Cabrera liked the speed of the trip. He would bring another detective with him.

There were ground rules, Cabrera told Boyd. Puente was not to be asked any questions about the case, the investigation, the bodies unearthed, or her arrest. "Ask her general stuff, anything that's not about any crimes," Cabrera said. "Or else I stop all questions for the rest of the flight."

Boyd agreed to the condition. He and the *Bee* would scoop every other news organization in the country just by carrying Puente on the plane.

Cabrera spent the time until the flight talking to the L.A. police at Rampart, then, when Puente was taken downtown to Parker Center, discussing her treatment. When she was brought to Rampart earlier in the evening, head down, hands cuffed in front of her, two women officers at her sides, Puente was bombarded by shouted questions from the swarm of TV reporters that followed the squad cars from the Royal Viking. Cabrera wanted to make sure Puente stayed in a cell, away from reporters, until he arrived to take custody.

He thought LAPD agreed. But instead, to satisfy the local media, the police "marched her back and forth to her cell," Cabrera said, annoyed, as he looked at the TV pictures. "Someone hit her on the head with a camera. Accidentally." During the garish exercise, Puente said nothing. Sometimes she had on a belly chain that kept her hands tightly at her sides or in front of her with restricted movement. She had been turned into a performing bear. The attention she had craved for so long—real lights, microphones, cameras—engulfed her, even reached out and struck her.

At 2:30 A.M. Puente was taken from her cell at Parker Center, wearing a bellychain, marching head down between uniformed women officers and detectives in lockstep. As she got out of an elevator to head for a squad car, a mass of reporters and cameras surged toward her. Then the whole clumsy parade backpedaled as she was hustled forward, several reporters tripping over each other to get out of the way.

She was put into a squad car, head pushed down awkwardly, clambering into the backseat, and rushed to the Learjet and the return trip to Sacramento waiting for her.

The original flight plan for the KCRA chartered jet was to Los Angeles International Airport. Boyd had the impression they would be on the ground for a while, long enough to get the local pictures he wanted.

At the last minute, the police changed the destination to Burbank. And Boyd was now informed they would be taking off again almost immediately.

He was startled by the speed and byzantine twists of the trip. He felt caught up in a maelstrom himself, like the police and Puente, unable to do much more than go along for the ride.

The Learjet touched down at Burbank airport in early morning blackness, lit only by the bright airport lights. As Boyd talked to Cabrera about what was going to happen, a truck began pumping jet fuel into the plane.

As if on cue, Puente appeared in her procession of squad cars, followed by cameras and reporters. She looked, to Boyd, wan, white-haired, ridiculous almost in her belly chain. She was formally transferred to the Sacramento detectives from LAPD, like a spy in a prisoner exchange. Boyd told his cameraman to get some shots of Puente being handed over.

Cabrera, who still smarted badly from her Saturday deception, believed he had some rapport with Puente. He said to her, "Are you ready to come home?"

She showed him the bump on her head from the camera. He asked, "Do you want anything, Dorothea? Tell me what you want to do now." It was not, Cabrera knew, a sincere question. He was taking her back no matter what she wished.

Puente, though, tired and sagging, her head low, said, "I want to go home."

Cabrera helped her into the jet. He mused about how she

had greeted him a few moments earlier, just like they had stepped from the porch of 1426 F inside for coffee.

Inside the jet, Cabrera sat by the window, his partner on the far side, Puente in the middle, also wearing a seat belt. The reporters sat opposite them. Cabrera advised Puente of her Miranda rights. She said nothing in reply, made no movement at all, a chained and seat belted granny. Her handcuffed hands lay in her lap as the jet took off.

The small passenger compartment was cramped and very loud with engine noise, and no one spoke for some time. The gaudy, colorful lights of Los Angeles slipped past below them in the darkness heading northward. It was about an hour flight time. Puente asked for a cup of coffee and got a half-filled plastic cup.

Boyd's cameraman began taping her and the *Bee's* photographer snapped off pictures. She peered out toward the window into the darkness, the random tiny city lights far below.

Gently, conversationally, Boyd began talking to her. He didn't know if she was guilty of anything, but he had been a reporter long enough to sense when someone was trying to use him. Puente a few moments before had initiated the chat. "I know you," she said to Boyd, long a local celebrity. "You probably know me. We've been acquaintances for a long time."

Puzzled, Boyd listened, nodded. He had never met her before, and he knew a con job when he heard it. She was trying to establish a friendly past for them both. He let her. They had, she said, been at some political and charitable functions together. They were, she seemed to imply, equal celebrities.

So, Boyd figured she'd broken the ice. He asked her, "How do you feel about going back to Sacramento? How do you feel now?"

His probing revitalized Puente. She spoke firmly suddenly, combatively. "I used to be a good person," she said, perhaps thinking back a long way to the halcyon days at 2100 F.

Then she turned to Cabrera, "I told you that. I have not killed anyone. The checks I cashed, yes." She repeated this several times to make sure everyone heard her, then lapsed back into silence, not even bothering to work Boyd or Cabrera anymore. She held the plastic cup and complained about being tired.

A little after 4:00 A.M. the jet landed at Sacramento Metropolitan Airport, and Puente was taken first to the police department for booking on the warrant charging her with Bert Montoya's murder, then to the orange and white block of the county jail. Boyd was fatigued, happy, delighted with the exclusive story he'd just gotten.

Cabrera, too, basked in momentary satisfaction that his misjudgment of Saturday had been blotted out by an efficient recapture of Puente. And she hadn't had time to commit any more crimes.

The early morning triumph turned sour almost as quickly, though, like so many illusions about Puente.

It was left to Cabrera's partner on the flight to sum up most people's reaction to Puente's capture. At the Burbank airport he said, "In twenty-three years of law enforcement, nothing is beyond the realm of believability when you're dealing with human beings."

He added with a nod, "We're relieved to get her off the streets."

19

THURSDAY MORNING, SACRAMENTO MUNICIPAL COURT, BEFORE Judge John Stroud, Dorothea Puente appeared in an orange jail jumpsuit, behind the railing guarding the jail tank. She held on to the railing for support and answered only two brief questions put to her by the judge: Was her name Dorothea Montalvo Puente? Yes, she said. Did she have the money to hire her own attorneys? No, she said.

The judge appointed two Sacramento County public defenders, Peter Vlautin and Kevin Clymo, to represent Puente. They conferred with her hastily at the railing, taking a copy of the one count murder complaint passed from the deputy DA to the clerk to the judge to them. Puente, Vlautin announced, would not enter any plea at that time. She had been arraigned by Judge Stroud on the single charge of killing Bert Montoya. Further investigation, more consultation were needed by her lawyers before she said whether she was guilty or not guilty.

Stroud set December 15 for her next court appearance.

Puente, tired, small, stout, was taken back into the tank.

The murmuring, fascinated courtroom turned to the normal cases that were called up in quick succession.

Left hanging in the air, just before Puente left the courtroom, was the announcement from the deputy DA that a new set of charges would be filed against her soon, charging her with all the murders she was believed to have committed.

In an almost angry bustle, Vlautin and Clymo hurried from the courtroom, followed by a line of reporters, stepping into the hallway, into another blaze of camera lights and shouted questions.

The overarching question on everybody's mind was just how many people had this white-haired woman killed?

Although it took only a few minutes, the arraignment in municipal court had been choreographed carefully. The judge ruled on requests for cameras in the courtroom, listened to the deputy DA in chambers officially state that new charges were coming, and then called Puente out of order on the busy morning calendar. Stroud had also made sure that two senior public defenders were ready to instantly take over Puente's representation. Although she had about $3,000 on her when she was arrested, everyone assumed Puente would claim indigency and be entitled to the free services of the county public defender.

California, almost alone in America, requires that two lawyers represent a defendant in a death penalty case. One lawyer puts on the defendant's case during the first part of the trial, the guilt phase. If the defendant is convicted, the jury must decide whether he dies in the gas chamber at San Quentin or is sentenced to life in prison without the possibility of parole. It is the sole job of the second lawyer to present mitigating evidence during this penalty phase of the trial.

Clymo would take charge of Puente's guilt phase defense, and Vlautin would try to keep her out of the gas chamber if she was convicted on multiple murder counts with special circumstances. Both men had been public defenders for over a decade and were familiar courtroom figures. Both had also earned a degree of respect from their adversaries in the DA's office.

It was assumed on Thursday morning that Tim Frawley would prosecute Puente, but O'Mara, as head of Major Crimes, could elect to keep her case and another serial killer trial for himself.

In the courthouse hallway, Vlautin made a good effort at mastering the stammer that afflicted him at times of stress. Red-faced, wearing black-rimmed glasses, with a receding hairline, looking more like a banker than a defense attorney, he spoke with greater authority than Puente's other lawyer, Clymo. Clymo, bald, his hair long and dangling in back, with a deep, slow voice and large, coarse frame, seemed a holdover from the sixties beside Vlautin.

They were thinking alike, though. It appeared they were embarking on a public relations campaign for Puente. During a series of press conferences they conducted throughout the trial, Vlautin and Clymo attacked the gaping unknowns in the case against Puente, and counter charged that she was being hustled through the legal system.

Vlautin, with Clymo towering beside him, worked himself into indignation over the media attention Puente was getting and the way the Sacramento police had carted her back to the capital.

"It's unheard of to have a suspect transported with reporters and cameras on the plane before she even has a chance to talk to an attorney."

Clymo broke in. Puente had "no opportunity to talk to anybody who had her interests in mind," he said.

"I don't know where the blame lies," Vlautin said, "but it isn't right." Puente, he said, had been upset and frightened since the ordeal.

The reporters and camera crews from all over the United States, France, and England, recorded the defense's irritation and paradoxical scorn for the "circus atmosphere" around Puente even as they fed it. "Our client denies killing anybody," Vlautin said clearly. "The true facts will come out in the courtroom, not in the courthouse hallway." He would subpoena everyone on the plane, all the film and videotape. The prosecution was so eager to get at Puente, Vlautin said, it had compromised the case against her. "I'm surprised she wasn't on the Geraldo Rivera show this morning," he snapped.

With a wave, more questions shouted after them, Puente's two lawyers strolled down the corridor, their first skirmish fought on her behalf.

Vlautin and Clymo were not alone in holding a press conference Thursday morning. A tired, visibly cranky Chief Kearns faced another ring of hostile reporters and cameras. He had been compelled to meet with some of them earlier, behind closed doors, to apologize for leaving them out of Puente's capture and flight back.

He was adamant in the press conference that he knew nothing about Cabrera's plan to use the KCRA jet. Several reporters were openly disbelieving that a lower-level police official, acutely aware of how bad the department looked after Saturday's escape, would take a major decision alone. But Kearns wouldn't budge. No one had told him about the flight beforehand. He wasn't responsible for any legal problems that developed.

"I'm ordering an inquiry into the matter. I'm not going to answer any more questions."

The only agency not heard from publicly was the DA. Frawley kept his own counsel as the week ended, and he tried to sort through the cascade of reports, files, and packages Puente's investigation created.

I went to see him, to urge him to file Ruth Munroe's murder against Puente.

He was a little weary, but cheered, his desk cluttered. The Coroner's office had just announced that the autopsies of two more F Street victims had been completed, without establishing a cause of death. The two still unidentified victims were described as an elderly woman, without teeth, dressed in a long-sleeved blouse, jacket, and low shoes. It was her body Enloe referred to on Monday, whose missing teeth the police thought they had found scattered below Puente's window. In fact, the police now believed the teeth were unconnected to Puente and had been deliberately put there merely to grab attention.

The second victim was a fifty-year-old woman, in a red blouse with narrow black stripes and another light-colored blouse over it.

The two victims underlined Frawley's problems. First, he still didn't know who these people were. The evidence collected from 1426 F might identify them, but for the moment, he was blind. He also had to worry that no cause of death would be listed. To convict Puente, it was essential that how she killed these people be discovered.

"You've got a cause of death in Munroe," I said when I saw him.

"It's kind of a weak case," he replied. "I'm looking at it."

I was very anxious, after the horror of what had happened, that Puente answer for Munroe.

We talked about using Munroe's cause of death, a drug overdose, to help explain what had happened to the other victims. It was a possibility.

Frawley was also exploring two other possible homicides to tie to Puente. One involved fleshy-lipped, doughy-faced Eugene Gamel, about to go on trial for child molestation in the summer of 1987. Gamel died in front of the F Street house, an apparent suicide, and Puente notified the police. It had definite echoes of Munroe's death.

"What's the other case?" I asked. Bodies seemed to turn up everywhere Puente went.

"It's a man she was going to marry," Frawley said.

"You're kidding."

"He lived with her at 1426 F for a while. The problem is to link him and a body they found a couple years ago."

Frawley had solved one mystery already, the smiling white-haired man in the photograph Cabrera seized from

Puente's dining room was Everson Gillmouth. The remaining mystery was why Puente kept his picture. Unless she thought she was above suspicion in his disappearance.

Frawley needed to connect Gillmouth's smiling photo with a John Doe body found in a makeshift coffin on the bank of the Sacramento River in January 1986.

20

EVERSON GILLMOUTH WAS A HAPPY MAN IN AUGUST 1985. HE was going to meet a woman he had been writing to for some time and he was going to marry her.

What happened to Gillmouth is tragic and horrible because it demonstrates that literally as soon as she got out of state prison, Dorothea Puente went right back to murder for profit.

Gillmouth was a lonely widower in his late seventies, a large-featured, avuncular looking man in glasses. He was the cousin who would come to holiday meals and not be seen for the rest of the year. He had retired from Martin Marietta, got a small pension from them, and lived for several years near his sister Reba and her husband in Sweet Home, Oregon.

He lived in an Airstream camper attached to a red Ford pickup truck. He did small jobs and for some time devoted himself to wood carving or leather working. Gillmouth's wood work was elaborate, totemistic, like the polished, intricate work of a tribesman. He exhibited and sold some of his work.

But living near his sister wasn't enough. Reba was also sturdy, large-framed, looking like she could run a frontier farm. She and Everson were not as close as they could have been, although she was very fond of him and proud of his talent.

Since his wife died, Gillmouth felt sour toward doctors, and although he was treated for significant heart problems and phlebitis, which required hospitalization, he never told Reba about it. When they both lived in Maryland in the seventies, they didn't see each other very much. It was from his loneliness that he parked his camper near Reba's home for several years.

He started writing to women in prison, too. He very much wanted to marry again, have a wife for his last years, and the intimacy of a home of his own. Gillmouth was a regular correspondent with a woman in an Oklahoma prison, and another in Banning, California. He offered to marry a woman prisoner in Oklahoma who had a child.

He also began writing to Dorothea Puente, then an inmate in Frontera. Their letters were friendly, then more personal, and Puente confessed to Gillmouth that she, too, wanted to settle down once more, straighten out her life and start anew with someone she could love.

They kept up this conversation by mail for a year, and Puente told Gillmouth that the prison would be releasing her to a halfway house in Fresno, California, for the last few months of her sentence. She was getting out early, after about three and a half years of the five-year sentence, because she had been an excellent prisoner and earned work credits, too.

Would Gillmouth like to meet her and the two of them could drive back to Sacramento? They could both live at her house on F Street. Puente had Gillmouth get in touch with Ricardo Odorica to set up the details of when to come to Fresno to pick her up.

Puente left the love struck Gillmouth with the clear belief she would become his second wife.

Gillmouth's sister Reba had read some of her brother's mail, so she knew about several of the women he was writing to. She did not, though, know about Dorothea until Everson told her. And startled her with the news that he was packing up his carvings, loading everything into the camper, and driving south to pick up his fiancée.

"If everything works out all right," Gillmouth happily told his sister, "Dorothea and I are going to get married."

Reba knew a little about Dorothea and did not share her brother's unabashed enthusiasm. It struck her as a risky, uncertain thing to end up in a strange city, no friends or family nearby, living with a woman he had never met.

But Everson was a very lonely man. When Reba saw him a few days later, he was in high spirits, looking forward to his new life.

It was the last time Reba ever saw her brother.

After Labor Day 1985, Reba thought she would hear from Everson about his arrival in Sacramento, what 1426 F Street was like or how he was getting along with Dorothea. Then more days passed without word. Knowing her brother was perhaps blinded to dangers by love, Reba called the Sacramento police, gave them Everson's new address and asked if they would go by and see if he was all right.

About September 17, police officers rang the doorbell at 1426 F Street and talked with Everson Gillmouth. He told them he was fine, there were no problems, they shouldn't have come out and bothered. He sounded peeved that his sister was checking up on him. He called Reba, complained about her worries and said the police had come by to see him. It was not a pleasant call.

It was the last time Reba heard Everson's voice.

She decided that if he wanted to be left alone, so be it.

Reba heard nothing more from Sacramento until October 14. She got her first letter from Puente. It was a sharpish note, annoyed that Reba had set the police on 1426 F Street. "Gill is staying at my house," Puente wrote. He was selling his carvings, too. He was angry with Reba, and "he doesn't want you to have the police out again." It ended, somewhat oddly, "Thinking of you."

A little over a week later, Reba got a second, much more chatty and cheery letter from Puente. It now sounded as though the two women had been friends for years. "Gill is busy with his carving, taking some down to Palm Springs to sell," Puente informed Reba. The bad news was that he had been "turned down by the Vets for assistance" and "his leg bothers him." They still planned on getting married in November.

The second letter was cozily signed, "Dorothea and Gill."

For a short time, Reba's vague suspicions about her brother and his new girlfriend ebbed.

Then, on November 2, 1985, Reba got a strange Mailgram. It was sent, purportedly, by Gillmouth. It said he was going to leave Dorothea. The wedding was off. He was planning on heading south.

Reba's fears flared up again. The wording, the tone, none of the Mailgram sounded like her brother had written it.

The Mailgram asked Reba not to try to stop him from taking the trip south. In his whole life, Everson had never asked her anything like that, nor had she ever tried to stop him from doing anything. But what could she do? Her brother had told her he didn't want to be checked up on, and the police had visited 1426 F Street and found everything in order.

Reba and her husband decided that Everson Gillmouth was obviously old enough to do as he pleased. It was interesting, though, that rather than call or write, Everson used a Mailgram, which bore no true sign he had written it.

There was a long, deep silence after that, and Reba worried about her brother.

Suddenly, in April 1986, she got a postcard from a woman named Irene. Irene wrote that she was Everson's new love. They had met during his travels. The postcard was chatty, like the letter Puente had sent. Irene told Reba, "We came to Sacramento to pick up the rest of Everson's things. He had a small stroke in January. I heard you had the police out." It was a peculiar reference, unless the postcard writer still felt nettled by Reba's concern for her brother.

She read on. Irene said that they had gone to the desert. "We're both health nuts," she gaily wrote, and Everson "has lost some weight." They also went to church every week. The card was signed, "Irene and Everson."

The whole thing—a new woman, the silence from Everson himself—was fishy, Reba thought. But she had no way of contacting her brother directly anymore. She hoped for the best and waited to hear from him.

Everson had actually gotten to 1426 F Street in mid-August 1985. He parked his camper and Ford pickup on the street until people complained, and then moved them a few blocks away.

His sole companion at 1426 F Street was Ricardo Odorica. The rest of the Odorica family lived in the south part of the city. Odorica was friendly and accommodating to Gillmouth, or Gill, as he called him. This man was about to marry Odorica's lady, the patroness of his family, the surrogate grandmother who so loved his wife and children.

Gill's excitement about meeting Dorothea for the first time mounted until September 9. He and Odorica drove to Fresno in his pickup. The three had a joyful, emotional reunion and drove back at once to Sacramento.

Gill and Dorothea set up housekeeping on the second floor at 1426 F. Odorica went on living on the first floor. After Gill had moved the pickup off the street, the two men took the Airstream camper to Odorica's sister's home in Lincoln for safekeeping. This was Dorothea's suggestion. She asked Ricardo if his sister had a place for the trailer while she and Gill ran a newspaper ad and sold it.

Everson Gillmouth was losing his worldly possessions to his future wife. Ricardo believed the gentleman had given the trailer to Dorothea as a gift. She herself had told him so.

Odorica liked Gill, who although much older than the lady, was courtly to her and dignified. He didn't see Gill very often, though, maybe once or twice a week. Odorica was working nights at the Clarion Hotel and sleeping during the day.

Gill seemed healthy for a man his age, even if he limped a little. He didn't complain about his health and the lady mothered him. In mid-December 1985, Odorica was preparing to make his annual Christmas trip to Mexico to see his father. One day, a little before he left, he saw Gill sitting in the front yard at 1426 F working on a wood carving. Gill, though, seemed in some pain, in his chest. Odorica had watched him take pills sometimes when he was having chest pains. But this time, when he told Gill he was going to the store, Gill didn't stop him, so the pains couldn't have been too bad.

In fact, the lady had once told him Gill was sick in bed, but that was the only time he reckoned Gill to be having physical difficulties of any importance.

Odorica left Sacramento, saying good bye to Gill and the lady, wishing them well. For some reason, the wedding seemed to be put off, November, then December, then no date. Gill looked tired, too.

Odorica got back on January 20, 1986. There was no one but the lady living at 1426 F Street. Where was Gill? Where had he gone? "He didn't like Sacramento," Puente told Odorica. "He went back to where he came from. He's gone back to Oregon."

The handyman, Ismael Florez, who had been doing paneling work around the house when Odorica left for Mexico, now had Gill's red Ford Pickup. "Gill sold it to him," Puente explained.

There was no further talk about Gill. He had left the lady. He no longer existed, as far as Odorica was concerned.

Shortly before Christmas 1985, right after Odorica had left the country and Gill and Puente lived alone at 1426 F Street, Jesus Meza stopped by to do a favor for his girlfriend.

Her name was Brenda Trujillo, and she was back in prison. When she was out, she lived at 1426 F off and on, was familiar with Puente, and left her belongings inside, too. Trujillo wanted Meza to pick up a box and some money.

Thin, dark-haired, a little twitchy, Meza was invited inside by Puente. They talked about Brenda, prison life, troubles.

Then white-haired, hard-faced Dorothea Puente told Meza she needed help. Meza, sitting in the upstairs living room with Puente, had noticed a pungent, unpleasant stink when he came inside. He didn't know what it was at first, but Puente's next words told him instantly.

"A man's died of a heart attack," Puente said calmly. "I don't know what to do with his body. I need help getting rid of it."

Meza was startled and disgusted. Puente said she'd pay him to take the body out, but he refused.

"Don't tell the police," Puente said, not quite begging and not quite ordering Meza.

"I won't. I won't," Meza promised, still shocked by the implication of this kindly-looking little old lady's words. A man was rotting somewhere nearby in the house.

As he left, in some haste, Meza recalled Puente's calm, her steely, bland conversation, her lack of concern about the things she was saying. As if having a dead man in the house was a garbage-disposal problem more than anything else.

Meza was determined it wasn't going to be his problem.

Ismael Florez, also dark-haired with a mustache, glum-looking most of the time, was drinking at the Rendezvous Club in downtown Sacramento, one night in September. A grand, almost regal-looking older woman swept in, ordered a drink. She sat with Florez. She needed someone to do work for her at 1426 F Street, she said.

He wanted to know what kind.

"General work, interior paneling, anything that needs to be fixed," she said.

Florez, who worked sometimes as a tile setter, knew basic carpentry, so he agreed. Over the next few months he nailed